# COOKING THE PORTUGUESE WAY
# IN SOUTH AFRICA

The first book of traditional Portuguese cooking to be published in South Africa in English – by **Mimi Jardim**, presenter of the television series *Bom Apetite*.

The Portuguese cuisine is surely one of the most distinctive and imaginative in the Western world. Much of its originality is derived from the exotic ingredients which the seafaring explorers of the fifteenth and sixteenth centuries brought back to their native shores – the pungent spices of the East and the tropical fruits of the New World – resulting in a colourful array of national and regional dishes.

While traditional Portuguese fare is redolent of the lavish use of garlic, olive oil and tomatoes, it is also characterised by unusual combinations of ingredients, and *Cooking the Portuguese Way in South Africa* offers more than 250 recipes that will challenge and inspire both the experienced and the novice cook: there is pork cooked with clams, prawns baked with brinjals and coconut milk, and chicken with pumpkin seeds. The Portuguese are ingenious in their use of left-overs: 'yesterday's bread', for example, is recycled to create the hearty and flavourful *açordas* (bread soups). Irresistible cakes and desserts using vast quantities of egg yolks, sugar, almonds and cinnamon are also included.

Mimi Jardim's recipes are animated by her vivacity and her enthusiasm for her subject, and there is something for everyone: new ideas for experienced and adventurous cooks, and encouraging advice for beginners.

**Mimi Jardim** was born in Portugal but completed her education in South Africa, where she graduated from the Teachers' Training College for Home Economics in Johannesburg.

She is well known in culinary circles in South Africa as a cookery demonstrator and teacher. She has lectured and taught home economics at colleges and schools, contributed articles on Portuguese cooking to newspapers and magazines, and for many years she ran her own school of Portuguese cooking.

# COOKING THE PORTUGUESE WAY
## IN SOUTH AFRICA

**Mimi Jardim**

With photographs by Paul Gordon

VIKING

# VIKING

Published by the Penguin Group
27 Wrights Lane, London W8 5TZ, England
Viking Penguin, a division of Penguin Books USA Inc, 375 Hudson Street,  New York, New York 10014, USA
Penguin Books Australia Ltd, Ringwood, Victoria, Australia
Penguin Books Canada Ltd, 2801 John Street, Markham, Ontario, Canada LR3 1B4
Penguin Books (NZ) Ltd, 182-190 Wairau Road, Auckland 10, New Zealand
Penguin Books, Amethyst Street, Theta Ext 1, Johannesburg, South Africa

Penguin Books Ltd, Registered Offices: Harmondsworth, Middlesex, England

First published in 1991
Reprinted in 1992

ISBN 0670 833 525

The moral right of the author has been asserted.

Designed by Graphicor
Typeset by GeeToo
Printed and bound by Tims Printing Co., Ltd.

**I dedicate this book to the male cooks in my family:**

my grandfather *(Avôzinho)*, my first cookery teacher
my father *(Vovô)*, an excellent cook
my husband (Papa), who is just as good
my sons – there are some lucky girls out there!
my son-in-law, who had no option but to learn the art
(otherwise no bride!)
my grandson, still too young to cook, but he enjoys his food

# Contents

# Prefácio

*Dar a conhecer a nossa cultura, as nossas tradições, é, sem dúvida, uma excelente maneira de viver Portugal no estrangeiro.*

*Desde que os primeiros emigrantes Portugueses se radicaram na África do Sul, constituindo hoje uma grande comunidade, trouxeram consigo as suas tradições passando-as a sucessivas gerações Luso-sul Africanas. Somos por essência um povo simples, corajoso, trabalhador, dotado de grande poder de adaptação e aculturação mas, especialmente muito hospitaleiros. A nossa maneira franca de receber os amigos está bem expressa na conhecida canção: É uma casa Portuguesa, concerteza, pão e vinho sobre a mesa . . .'*

*Estando os Portugueses ligados às navegações, às descobertas de outras terras, à vivência com outros povos, não é de estranhar que a nossa culinaria seja por vezes exótica, contendo condimentos que a tornaram internacionalmente conhecida e afamada.*

*Mimi Jardim, autora do primeiro livro de receitas Portuguesas editado em língua inglesa na África do Sul, é bem conhecida na arte de culinária. O seu livro, para além de dar a oportunidade de podermos executar em nossas casas as tradicionais iguarias Portuguesas, proporciona um melhor conhecimento do nosso país, uma vez que, em muitos deles a autora introduziu, num estilo simples mas gracioso como ela própria, lendas e histórias do nosso imaginário colectivo.*

*Vera Coutinho*
**Vera Coutinho**
**Licenciada em Filologia Românica (Universidade do Porto)**
**Delegada do Instituto de Apoio à Emigracão e Comunidades Portuguesas em Joanesburgo**

# Preface

The sharing of our culture and traditions is without doubt the best way of keeping the Portuguese heritage alive for those of us who live abroad.

The first Portuguese emigrants who settled in South Africa brought with them the traditions which have been passed on to successive generations of what is now a large community of *Luso* South Africans. The Portuguese are essentially a hard-working people of simplicity and courage who have the ability to adapt both socially and culturally to their environment. But their strongest characteristic is their warm hospitality. The open way in which the Portuguese receive their friends is clearly expressed in the words of a well-known song: *É uma casa Portuguesa, concerteza, pão e vinho sobre a mesa . . .'*

Given their long seafaring history, the discovery of new lands and their experience of living with people of different cultures and traditions, it is not surprising that the Portuguese cuisine sometimes appears to be rather exotic containing, as it does, the distinctive ingredients that have made it internationally well known.

Mimi Jardim, author of the first Portuguese cookbook to be written in English in South Africa, is a familiar name in the world of cookery. Her book not only gives us the opportunity to try out traditional Portuguese recipes at home, but the introductions to many of the recipes give charming insights into old Portuguese traditions and legends and enhance our knowledge of the country itself.

**Vera Coutinho**

# Acknowledgements

In the compilation of a book of this nature, help, advice, time, patience and encouragement are provided by far too many people to name individually. But they know who they are and I thank them all most sincerely.

I express my special appreciation to the following:

my family, friends and pupils for their contributions;
my father for assisting me with all the 'oldies';
my husband for his invaluable advice and help with the styling;
Paul Gordon for his patience, understanding (and tasting!) during the photo sessions;
Terry, Suzi and Ana-Bela for endless hours of work on the manuscript;
Gaby and Bella for their encouragement and constructive criticism;
Mr Gilberto Leal for the beautiful ceramic tiles;
Frontline Office Equipment for attending so promptly to my frequent SOS messages from the computer room;
Pam for her careful editing and for the fun we had discussing the recipes;
and last, but by no means least, Alison for her confidence – I hope the waiting has been worth while.

# Introduction

For some unknown reason, Portuguese cooking has not been explored as deeply as that of its European cousins. It is a cuisine rich in culinary traditions and many dishes owe their origins to the course of Portugal's history, most notably the discoveries of its early explorers. Indeed, the exotic side of Portuguese cooking is indebted to those voyages of discovery: spices were brought from India, oranges from China, and Brazil, Mozambique and Angola provided coffee.

Many South Africans were first introduced to Portuguese cooking on visits to Angola and Mozambique and dishes such as chicken piri piri, grilled prawns, *prego* rolls and calamari are well known. But what about the rest of Portuguese cooking? Unless you have Portuguese friends or neighbours you will, unfortunately, not know much about it. Even Portuguese restaurants serve a very limited selection of Portuguese dishes – and they have opted for the quick-and-easy and well-known ones.

For many years now I have held my Portuguese cooking classes in Johannesburg, but I have longed to share my recipes and my cultural heritage with the rest of South Africa. I hope that this book will encourage you to try cooking the Portuguese way and that you will have as much fun in the kitchen as I had in selecting the recipes.

Some of the recipes are easy, some are a little more adventurous, and others are ones that have become famous over the years. Some readers may feel that there are omissions, but it was impossible to include *everything*.

**Mimi Jardim**

*Provinces of Mainland*
# PORTUGAL

MINHO

• Bragança

• Braga

TRÁS-OS-MONTES E
ALTO DOURO

Vila Real •

DOURO
LITORAL

Porto •

*Douro River*

BEIRA ALTO

• Aveiro

• Viseu

• Guarda

• Coimbra

BEIRA
LITORAL

BEIRA BAIXA

Abrantes •

• Castelo Branco

Nazaré •

S P A I N

*Tagus River*

ESTREMADURA

A T L A N T I C   O C E A N

• Santarém

Sintra •

RIBATEJO

Estremoz •

• Elvas

LISBON

ALTO
ALENTEJO

• Évora

• Beja

BAIXO
ALENTEJO

ALGARVE

Sagres •

• Albufeira

• Faro

# A Brief Guide to Portugal

To appreciate and understand Portuguese cooking, you need to know a little about the country and its people. (No, I am not embarking on a geography lesson.)

Portugal is a small country situated in the south-western corner of Europe. Have you ever been to the Kruger National Park? Well, that is how big we are! One of our poets called Portugal 'the garden beside the sea' *(jardim a beira-mar plantado)*. Portugal is three times as long as it is wide and its entire western and southern limits are bathed by the sea. This probably has something to do with our love of fish and seafood.

There are eleven provinces in Portugal, each with its own climate, customs, and distinctive culinary specialities. It has been written that the saints are from the north, the poets from the centre and the navigators from the south, and a well-known proverb describes the main characteristics of some of its people:

> Lisbon plays
> Coimbra studies
> Braga prays
> Oporto works

In the northern provinces the colourful costumes of the people present a strong contrast to the rugged countryside. They prepare delicious sausages and nourishing stews and offer their guests a warm welcome. Central Portugal has a romantic air, contributed to by university students, monasteries and cosy inns. Here you will find such delicacies as suckling pig and numerous egg-yolk sweets. As befits a capital city, in Lisbon you will find dishes from all the different provinces – *iscas* (marinated liver) and grilled sardines are among the favourites. The Alentejo bread is famous and is used in many dishes, and this arid area also provides most of the country's cork. The golden beaches of the Algarve have turned it into a tourist paradise. Figs, almonds, and endless varieties of fish provide many a gourmet meal. The islands of Madeira and the Azores complete the menu with their exotic tropical fruits.

# Portuguese Cooking in South Africa

Gone are the days when ingredients for Portuguese cooking had to be smuggled in from neighbouring countries. Portuguese delicatessens and fisheries have mushroomed in recent years, particularly in the large cities. Although some of the ingredients are still imported, most of them are readily available. If you become addicted to Portuguese cooking, I suggest that you plant a lemon tree and a bay tree without delay and do some serious growing of herbs such as parsley and coriander, and don't forget the chillies (piri piri) and kale leaves.

The following ingredients are basic to Portuguese cooking:

* Salted dried cod *(bacalhau)* is obtainable whole or sliced. It needs to be soaked for 12 – 24 hours before use. See p30 for details.
* Smoked ham *(presunto)* is used as a snack and in stews. Bacon may be substituted if *presunto* is not available.
* Smoked sausage *(chouriço)* is eaten as a snack and also used to enhance the flavour of certain dishes.
* Olive oil *(azeite)* and both green and black olives.
* Garlic is used extensively in traditional Portuguese cooking. Each clove is usually crushed lightly with the back of a knife – removal of the skin is optional. Some recipes stipulate that the garlic cloves be left whole, or they may occasionally be chopped or pressed.
* Chick peas (dried or tinned) and black-eyed beans.
* Tomatoes are an essential ingredient in many meat, poultry and fish dishes. Most recipes require that they be skinned, seeded and chopped, which is a messy and time-consuming business. **Try my corner-cutting method of grating tomatoes:** take a whole tomato in your hand and grate it carefully on the coarse side of your cheese grater. You will be left with the tomato skin in your hand and a lovely tomato purée on the plate, ready for use in any *refogado.*

# Herbs and spices used
# in Portuguese cooking

The Portuguese seafaring explorers of the fifteenth and sixteenth centuries established a flourishing trade with the East and brought many exotic spices – curry, cinnamon, cloves, nutmeg, pepper – directly to Portugal enabling the cooks of those days to experiment with many new flavours. A few have remained firm favourites down the centuries.

✳ Aniseed, whole and powdered
✳ Bay leaf, whole, powdered or crushed
✳ Cinnamon, stick or powdered
✳ Cloves
✳ Coriander, especially fresh coriander leaves
✳ Cumin powder
✳ Mint
✳ Nutmeg
✳ Oregano
✳ Paprika *(colorau)*
✳ Piri piri (called *gindungo* in Angola) is a small, exceedingly hot chilli imported from Africa and now almost synonymous with Portuguese cooking. Piri piri can be obtained as whole, dried chillies, as powder and as a sauce. Some of my recipes state 'piri piri to taste' and, because it is so very hot, I suggest that you start with one or two whole chillies and see how your tastebuds respond before adding more. Two or three whole piri piri are equivalent to about 1,5 ml of the powdered chilli. (Before you set your palate on fire, make sure you have an abundant supply of *vinho verde* . . . )

White and red wine are both used frequently in Portuguese cooking, as are Port and Madeira wines.

# Food for Special Occasions

A Portuguese meal usually starts with a soup, followed by a main course of meat or fish, with fresh fruit for dessert. Apart from salads, rice or potatoes, side dishes are not usually served. Coffee is a must at the end of a meal, and is taken either at home or at the nearest café (a good opportunity to meet the neighbours and catch up with the day's news).

## Christmas

Christmas Eve supper is still a very important family gathering in most parts of Portugal. Although the dishes served vary from region to region, the following are usually included:

| | |
|---|---|
| salt cod | assorted fritters |
| roast turkey | rice pudding |
| suckling pig | King's Crown Cake |
| tipsy slices | honey cake |

## For a buffet

| | |
|---|---|
| party rice | tuna vinaigrette |
| prawn rissoles | lupins |
| cod fish cakes | assorted pastries |
| meat croquettes | crème caramel |
| chicken piri piri | |

# Appetisers and Snacks
## *Acepipes e Petiscos*

Visitors to a Portuguese home are always

greeted with a smile and a glass of wine.

*Petiscos* are usually served with the wine and

sometimes more elaborate snacks *(acepipes)*

are prepared.

# Cod Fish Cakes
## *Pastéis de Bacalhau*

These are a must at any Portuguese function. They may be served hot but, because they can be prepared in advance, they are usually eaten cold. Salt cod is so expensive that it is tempting to mix a small amount of it with other varieties of fish. This will alter the flavour completely and any true Portuguese palate will detect the difference at once.

See p30 for details on the preparation and storage of *bacalhau*.

| | |
|---|---|
| 500 g *bacalhau* | 2 – 3 eggs |
| 1 kg potatoes | salt and pepper |
| 1 onion, chopped | piri piri (optional) |
| 12,5 ml chopped parsley | oil for frying |

Boil the fish in water for 15 – 20 minutes. Drain and remove the skin and bones. Place the fish in a food processor and using the metal blade process until it resembles threads. Place the flaked fish in a large bowl. (Before the days of food processors this step was usually accomplished by placing the fish in a dish cloth and rubbing it until it was completely mashed.)

Boil the potatoes in their skins. When cooked, peel and mash and add to the fish. Add the chopped onion and parsley. Add the eggs one at a time, mixing well. The mixture should be quite stiff – 2 or 3 eggs will be needed, depending on their size. Adjust the seasoning.

Using two spoons, roll the mixture into oval-shaped cakes. Fry in hot oil until golden brown. Drain on absorbent paper. Serve hot with a salad, or cold as a snack.

Makes about four dozen. (I don't guarantee that they will all reach the table.)

**Variation**
Fry the onion in 10 ml olive oil until golden. Add the fried onions and oil to the fish mixture. Separate the eggs and after adding the yolks, fold in the stiffly beaten egg whites.

# Cod Fish Fritters
## *Pataniscas de Bacalhau*

These resemble small crumpets. Although *bacalhau* is the fish of choice for this recipe, any other cooked fish or even tinned tuna fish can be used instead, as can a mixture of chopped cold meats or vegetables. It is a great recipe for using up left-overs. It makes a delicious lunch dish, served with a lettuce salad or a black-eyed bean salad.

250 g *bacalhau*
250 g flour
15 ml olive oil or cooking oil
salt and pepper
3 eggs
100 ml white wine

cold water
15 ml chopped parsley
5 ml chopped coriander leaves
  (optional)
1 onion, chopped
oil for shallow frying

Soak the fish as described on p30. Flake the fish after removing the bone and skin. For this dish it is not necessary to cook the *bacalhau* first.

Sift the flour into a large bowl. Make a well in the centre and add the oil, seasonings, eggs and wine and enough cold water to make a soft batter. Add the flaked fish, parsley, coriander and chopped onion and mix well. Drop tablespoons of batter into hot oil and fry (4 or 5 at a time) on both sides until golden brown. Drain on kitchen paper and serve at once.

**Serves 4 – 6.**

# Prawn Patties
## *Rissois de Camarão*

Served at every party, these patties are also good as a lunch-time snack whether it's in the streets of Lisbon or down-town Johannesburg. Do not be put off by the length of the recipe – they are worth the effort. Invite a friend to join you in an afternoon of rissole-making and share the results. They also freeze well.

### *Filling*
500 g cooked prawns (reserve
   the cooking water)
10 ml salt
5 ml olive oil
10 ml butter
1 onion, chopped
1 small tomato, skinned and
   finely chopped or grated
1 clove garlic, crushed
2 ml lemon juice
5 ml chopped parsley
piri piri to taste

### *Pastry dough*
250 ml water
salt
25 ml butter
250 ml flour

### *Coating*
beaten egg
breadcrumbs
oil for frying

### *White sauce*
25 ml butter
25 ml flour
250 ml liquid (made up of the
   prawn water and milk)
2 egg yolks

Boil the prawns in water and salt. Reserve the cooking water. Shell the prawns and cut them in half.

Fry the onion in the butter and oil. Add the tomato, garlic, lemon juice, parsley, and salt and piri piri to taste. Cook for 5 – 10 minutes until soft. Stir in the prawns.

Make the white sauce following the recipe given on p121. Add the prawn mixture to the sauce. Taste and adjust the seasoning. Allow to cool.

Meanwhile make the pastry dough. Bring the water, salt and butter to the boil. Remove from the heat and add the sifted flour. Beat well. Return to the heat and cook for 5 minutes or until the dough comes away from the pan. Cool. Roll out on a floured board. Cut small pastry rounds and place one teaspoonful of the prawn mixture on the lower half of each circle. Fold and seal each pastry round, dip in beaten egg and breadcrumbs and fry in deep fat until golden brown. Uncooked, these patties can be frozen for up to three months.

**Variations**

✳ Tuna rissoles – substitute one tin of tuna for the prawns.
✳ *Bacalhau* – substitute 250 ml cooked shredded *bacalhau* for the prawns.
✳ Clams – substitute one tin of baby clams for the prawns.

# Sardine Pâté

| | |
|---|---|
| 2 tins Portuguese sardines | 12,5 ml chopped onion |
| 5 ml tomato sauce | 1 clove garlic |
| 5 ml mustard | 125 g cream cheese |
| 10 ml lemon juice | salt and pepper |
| 60 g soft butter | 1 ml piri piri sauce |
| 5 ml chopped parsley | |

Drain the sardines and place in a food processor. Add the rest of the ingredients and process until smooth. Taste and adjust seasonings if necessary.

Chill for one hour before serving. Serve with toasted slices of Portuguese rolls.

# Pickled Tuna and Pickled Octopus

## *Atum de Escabeche, Polvo de Escabeche*

### *TUNA*

| | |
|---|---|
| 500 g fresh tuna | *Marinade* |
| 1 small onion | 125 ml olive oil |
| 2 cloves garlic | 100 ml vinegar |
| 1 sprig of parsley | 1 small onion, chopped |
| salt | 4 cloves garlic, chopped |
| 10 ml olive oil | 10 ml chopped parsley |
| | 5 ml fresh coriander, chopped |
| | salt, pepper, and piri piri to taste |

Place the tuna in a saucepan of boiling water. Add the whole onion and garlic, parsley, salt and olive oil. Boil until the tuna is tender – about 10 – 15 minutes. Drain the tuna, reserving 125 ml of the liquid.

Mix all the ingredients for the marinade with the reserved liquid. Cut the tuna into small pieces and add to the mixture. Refrigerate for at least 24 hours before using.

### OCTOPUS

Octopus may be bought either fresh or frozen. Wash the octopus several times. Then, holding the octopus by the head, lower it into a saucepan of boiling water and remove. Repeat this five times, making sure that the water is boiling each time. This procedure will tenderise the octopus.

Now proceed as in the preparation of pickled tuna.

# Drumsticks
## *Coxinhas de Galinha*

One of my Brazilian favourites.

| *Filling* | *Coating* |
|---|---|
| 1 medium chicken, stewed | flour |
| | beaten egg |
| *Pastry dough* | breadcrumbs |
| as for Prawn Patties above | oil for frying |

Stew the chicken in a tomato-based sauce (try the recipe on p120). Debone, reserving the sauce and some of the bones.

Make the pastry dough. Roll small pieces of dough in your hands. Make a hole in the centre of each ball of dough, fill with stewed chicken and a little sauce and close over. Place a small chicken bone at one end of each ball, close the pastry around the bone and shape into a drumstick. Dip into flour, beaten egg and breadcrumbs. Adjust the shape if necessary. Refrigerate for 30 minutes and then deep-fry in hot oil.

# Chicken Giblets or Livers
## *Pipis de Galinha*

This recipe must have been devised to use up all the giblets left over from home-slaughtered chickens. Nowadays chickens are bought from supermarkets and they rarely come with giblets. Chicken livers can be bought separately, either fresh or frozen. You can use both giblets and livers in this recipe, or one or the other. However, the cooking time for giblets is longer than that for livers. Giblets need 15 – 20 minutes, but the livers should be added only 5 – 8 minutes before serving. Have lots of fresh bread and rolls on hand to dip into the sauce.

1 kg chicken giblets or
   chicken livers
20 ml olive oil
10 ml spices (2 ml ground
   cumin, 1 ml ground cloves,
   5 ml paprika, 1 bay leaf,
   salt, pepper, whole or
   ground piri piri to taste)

2 onions, chopped
2 cloves garlic, crushed
100 ml white wine

Fry the giblets or livers in the olive oil until brown. Add the spices and seasonings and stir well. Add the chopped onion and garlic. Fry for 5 minutes. Add the wine and simmer gently until cooked. If you are cooking giblets only, a little water may be added if necessary.
**Serves 4 – 6.**

# Meat Croquettes
## *Croquetes de Carne*

Another party favourite, making use of left-over roast meat.

250 g pot roast, minced
   (see recipe for *Carne*
   *Estufada* on p62)
50 ml gravy
salt and pepper
piri piri to taste
2 ml ground nutmeg
15 ml Port wine
5 ml lemon juice
2 egg whites

1 whole egg
breadcrumbs
oil for frying

*White sauce*
30 g butter
30 g flour
100 ml milk
2 egg yolks

Place the mince in a mixing bowl. Add enough strained gravy to moisten the meat. Make a thick white sauce (see recipe on p121) and add the seasonings, piri piri, nutmeg, Port wine and lemon juice. Add the sauce to the meat and mix well. The mixture will resemble a thick dough. Sprinkle with breadcrumbs to avoid drying out. Cover and place in a refrigerator or cool place until the mixture can be easily handled.

Place the mixture on a floured board and mould into croquettes using a knife to flatten the ends. Beat the egg whites together with the whole egg. Dip the croquettes into the egg mixture and then into the breadcrumbs. Reshape if necessary.

Place the croquettes on a tray lined with paper towel and cover. Refrigerate for 2 – 3 hours. Deep-fry in oil over a medium heat until golden brown.

### Variation

Roll out puff or flaky pastry. Cut into round shapes with a pastry cutter. Place 5 ml of the meat mixture in the centre of each round. Using a pastry brush, wet the edges of the pastry and fold over to form half-moon shapes. Deep-fry in hot oil until golden brown. Eat while hot.

# Broad Beans in Vinaigrette Sauce
## *Fava Rica*

Traditionally the street-vendors of Lisbon – especially the women – used to carry their goods on their heads and shout their wares at the tops of their voices. It was part of a housewife's daily routine to gather round the vendors, greeting neighbours and exchanging gossip. Besides *fava rica*, the street vendors sold a multitude of other things – fish, water, newspapers, bread, lupins – and also offered services such as the sharpening of knives or the repairing of household utensils. Unfortunately modern life has made the services of the street vendor redundant and this colourful aspect of daily life has faded away.

| | |
|---|---|
| 500 g dried broad beans | 20 ml olive oil |
| 6 cloves garlic, whole | salt and pepper |
| 10 ml chopped coriander leaves | 10 ml vinegar |

Soak the beans overnight. Next day place the beans in a saucepan, add enough water to cover, and cook until tender. Add salt just before they are cooked. Drain. Add the rest of the ingredients and toss lightly. Serve hot, or cold as a salad.

**Serves 6 – 8.**

# Garlic Almonds
## *Amêndoas com Alho*

20 g unsalted butter
3 – 5 cloves garlic, crushed
salt and whole piri piri to taste
200 g almonds

Place the butter in an ovenproof dish and add the garlic and piri piri. Place the dish in an oven preheated to 180° C for 5 minutes, and then remove the garlic and piri piri. Add the almonds to the dish and toss them in the hot butter. Return the dish to the oven for 10 – 15 minutes, until the almonds are brown – watch them carefully. Remove from the oven and sprinkle the almonds with salt. Serve hot or cold.

# Curried Cashew Nuts
## *Caju com Caril*

20 g unsalted butter
5 ml curry powder
salt and piri piri to taste
125 g unsalted cashew nuts

Melt the butter in a frying pan. Add the curry, piri piri and salt. Fry the nuts in the butter until golden. Drain on paper and serve.

# Pumpkin Seeds
## *Pevides*

Wash pumpkin seeds and boil in salted water for 10 minutes. Drain. Place in a roasting tray and dry in a slow oven.

# Fried Broad Beans
## *Fava Frita*

Soak dried beans for 24 hours. Remove the skins and cut in half. Drain well in kitchen paper. Fry in oil for approximately 10 minutes. Drain. Sprinkle well with salt and pepper or piri piri.

# Fried Chick Peas
## *Grão Frito*

Soak the chick peas overnight. Rub them together to remove the skins. Proceed as for Fried Broad Beans above.

# Roasted Chestnuts
## *Castanhas Assadas*

Chestnuts are symbolic of Autumn, Sao Martinho and new wine. The roasted-chestnut vendors on every street corner are a sign that winter is on the way. Chestnuts are sold piping-hot and wrapped in newspaper. Buy a packet of six at one street corner and eat them until you reach the next street corner and then buy another packet. By now you will be thirsty, but I won't tell you what to do . . .

Traditionally chestnuts are roasted by the fire at night in a special earthenware pot with holes in its sides, but you will probably have to rely on your electric oven.

Score each chestnut across its width. Wash and place in a roasting pan and sprinkle with lots of coarse salt. Place in a very hot oven and roast. Don't forget the *água pé*.

# Quick Assorted Snacks
## *Acepipes Variados*

✳ Slices of smoked ham *(presunto)* with olives.

✳ Cottage cheese and sliced quince jam *(marmelada)*.

✳ A variety of canned Portuguese fish and seafood is available locally, such as tuna, sardines, squid, cuttlefish, mackerel and octopus. Serve with slices of lemon, olives and Portuguese rolls – and don't forget the wine!

✳ Grilled Portuguese sausage *(chouriço assado)*. Place a tot of Portuguese brandy in a heat-proof container. Light the brandy and, using two forks, hold the sausage over the flame. Special 'piggy-shaped' containers for this recipe can be obtained locally.

# Soups
## *Sopas*

According to *The Book of Food* published by

P M S Hand in 1927, a woman who cannot make

soup should not be allowed to marry.

Can you imagine having soup twice a day, every

day, for as long as you can remember? In

Portuguese homes soup is traditionally served at

every meal – light soups in summer and more

substantial ones in winter. In the north of Portugal

soup is sometimes eaten after the main course.

Some say it helps 'wash down' the heavy meal.

# Stone Soup
## *Sopa de Pedra*

Have you ever tasted Stone Soup? There is a legend attached to this recipe. The main character in the legend varies from a beggar to a monk to a shepherd. The ingredients also vary, but you *must* have the stone.

A very hungry man knocked at a farmer's door late one night, begging for food. The mealtime had long passed and there were no left-overs. The man, who held a gleaming stone in his hand, asked if he might make some simple requests. 'I must have a pot with some water and a fire.' These were provided. He placed the stone in the pot and then said: 'This will taste better with a little olive oil and salt.' These were brought to him. As the water boiled, the man looked at his hosts and remarked, 'I am sure you would like to taste my soup. Perhaps the flavour will be improved if we add some bacon or sausage or vegetables.' These were duly provided. As the soup simmered the man enchanted the family with tales of his travels. In due course wine and cheese were placed on the table and everyone ate the soup until there was nothing left but the stone. The man washed the stone, placed it in his pocket, thanked his hosts and disappeared into the night.

This is my version of the soup – without the stone! You may add a stone if you like but I will guarantee no difference in the flavour.

| | |
|---|---|
| 250 g butter beans or sugar beans, soaked overnight | 1 bay leaf |
| 100 g *chouriço* | 5 ml paprika |
| 500 g pork shank | 1 carrot |
| 100 g beef short ribs | 1 turnip |
| 12,5 ml olive oil | 2 medium potatoes |
| 1 onion, cut in half | 250 g pumpkin |
| 1 tomato | 2 – 3 kale leaves *or* 250 ml cabbage, chopped |
| ½ small green pepper, chopped | salt and pepper |
| 1 clove garlic | 250 ml elbow macaroni |

Place the drained beans and the meats in a large pot and cover with water. Add the oil, onion, tomato, green pepper, garlic, bay leaf and paprika. Simmer until almost cooked – about 2 hours.

Meanwhile, prepare the vegetables. Chop the carrot and turnip. Dice the potatoes and pumpkin. Shred or thinly slice the cabbage. Add all the vegetables to the soup. Add the salt and pepper. Simmer for 1 ½ hours. Add the macaroni and adjust the seasoning.

This is a very thick soup. It tastes even better if it is made a day in advance of serving. My mother used to add soaked dried chestnuts and sometimes tiny fig-sized pears.

**Serves 4 – 6.**

# Kale Soup
## *Caldo Verde*

This recipe has its origins in the north of Portugal. The colour of the soup reminds the Portuguese of the Costa Verde region. It reminds my children of grass (and that is why they call it 'grass soup'). A special type of cabbage is used in this soup. Almost every Portuguese in South Africa grows it in his garden. The leaves can be bought ready sliced from Portuguese fisheries and delis. Kale or tender cauliflower leaves can also be used. If all else fails, knock at the door of any Portuguese friend and ask for a few leaves – I do it all the time. If *chouriço* (Portuguese sausage) is not available, use quartered salami slices.

| | |
|---|---|
| 1 kg potatoes, sliced | 20 – 25 ml olive oil |
| 2 onions, sliced | 6 – 8 kale leaves *or* 1 packet |
| 1 clove garlic | sliced cabbage |
| 1,5 litres water | sausage *(chouriço)* |
| salt | |

Boil the potatoes, onions and garlic in the water. When they are almost cooked, add the salt and olive oil. Mash or purée the potatoes, onion and garlic and return them to the saucepan. Add more water if necessary and bring to the boil.

Shred the cabbage leaves by placing 2 – 3 leaves together, rolling them tightly, and then cutting into thin slices with a very sharp knife. (Or shred the leaves in a food processor: feed the rolled leaves into the tube and use the slicing blade.) Add the cabbage to the boiling soup and cook for 5 – 10 minutes – the leaves should remain crisp.

Slice the sausage and place 2 – 3 slices into individual bowls. Pour the hot soup over the sausage. Serve with slices of mealie bread *(broa)*.

**Serves 4 – 6.**

# Sopa 'O Que Sai'

When we first came to South Africa we used to buy a tickey's worth of soup greens and have vegetables for the whole week . . . turnips, carrots, cabbage, parsley, celery, spinach. This is a recipe for a soup which my dad used to prepare. It was unfamiliar to us and we asked him what it was. He answered, *'O que sai'*, meaning 'We will eat whatever the finished product is'. I call it 'cleaning-the-fridge soup'.

| | |
|---|---|
| 200 g beef shin | 2 carrots, coarsely chopped |
| 1 tomato, chopped | 250 ml cabbage, chopped |
| 1 onion, chopped | 1 stick celery, chopped |
| 1 clove garlic, crushed | 250 ml pumpkin, cubed |
| 20 ml olive oil | 100 ml chopped parsley |
| salt and pepper to taste | 250 ml macaroni |
| 2 turnips, coarsely chopped | |

Place the meat in a pot and cover with water. Add the tomato, onion, garlic, oil and seasonings and simmer until the meat is tender. Add the chopped vegetables and cook until soft. Lastly, add the macaroni and when that is cooked adjust the seasonings and serve.

**Serves 4 – 6.**

# Everyday Soup
## Sopa do Dia

How can anyone possibly serve a different soup twice a day, every day of the year? Many variations and adaptations have to be devised. Here is a little help.

| | |
|---|---|
| 1 stick celery | 1 clove garlic |
| 2 turnips | 100 g pumpkin (optional) |
| 2 carrots | 10 ml olive oil |
| 1 tomato | 200 g butter |
| 1 onion | water *or* chicken stock |
| 2 potatoes | salt and pepper |

Wash and chop the vegetables and then sauté them in the oil and butter. Add enough water or chicken stock to cover the vegetables and boil until they are tender. Place in a liquidiser and blend to a purée-like consistency. Return to the pan, adding more water if necessary. Adjust the seasoning and then add one of the following flavourings:

- ✳ sliced green beans
- ✳ turnip greens
- ✳ shredded cabbage
- ✳ watercress
- ✳ purslane
- ✳ snowpeas
- ✳ chopped spinach
- ✳ shredded lettuce – it's delicious

The purée may be frozen in portions and used when required. The above quantities will serve 4 – 6.

# Tomato Soup
## *Sopa de Tomate*

2 kg ripe tomatoes, chopped
2 carrots, chopped
1 onion, chopped
1 turnip, chopped
1 kg potatoes, diced
25 ml olive oil

1,5 litres water
salt and pepper
4 eggs
sliced Portuguese rolls
10 ml garlic butter (see p124)
chopped parsley to garnish

Sauté the vegetables in the olive oil. Add the water and simmer until the vegetables are tender. Add the seasoning. Purée the soup in a blender, adding more water if necessary. The consistency should be that of thin cream. Just before serving poach the eggs in the soup.

To serve, place slices of bread spread with garlic butter in soup bowls, top with a poached egg, add the soup and sprinkle with chopped parsley.

**Serves 4.**

# Chick Pea Soup
## *Puré de Grão*

500 g chick peas
1 onion, sliced or quartered
1 clove garlic
1 turnip, sliced or quartered

1 medium potato
25 ml olive oil
salt and pepper
turnip tops or tender spinach

Soak the chick peas overnight. Drain, place in a pot and cover with boiling water. Add the onion, garlic, turnip and potato and simmer until tender. Place in food processor or liquidiser and blend until smooth. Add the olive oil and the seasonings. Pour the liquidised soup back into the pot, add the shredded turnip tops and boil, uncovered, for 5 minutes. Serve with croûtons.

**Serves 4 – 6.**

# Fennel Soup
## *Sopa de Funcho*

Fennel is used abundantly on the islands of Madeira and the Azores. Funchal, the capital of Madeira, derives its name from the word *funcho*. This particular recipe is very typical of the Azores. Usually only the leaves of the fennel are used, leaving the bulbs for salads or for braising, but I use the whole plant. Beans-in-the-pod (that is, before they are dried) are seasonally available but are a little difficult to find unless you grow your own, so I use dried beans. This soup is best made a day in advance.

|   |   |
|---|---|
| 250 g spare-ribs | 500 ml fennel |
| 20 ml coarse salt | pepper to taste |
| 100 g bacon, diced | 2 potatoes, roughly chopped |
| 50 g *chouriço*, sliced | chopped cabbage (optional) |
| 250 g dried beans, soaked overnight *or* 500 g beans-in-the-pod | |

Sprinkle the spare-ribs with the salt and leave for 3 – 4 hours. Wash well and then cut into pieces. Place the meats and drained beans in a pot and cover with water. Boil until both are cooked and then add the remaining ingredients. Continue cooking until the potato and fennel are soft. If you would like a thick broth, remove some of the beans and potatoes, mash them and then return them to the pot.

For vegetarians, the meats may be omitted altogether and 15 ml olive oil added instead.

**Serves 4 – 6.**

# Chestnut Soup
## *Sopa de Castanhas Piladas*

If you fancy something unusual, try this. In the old days the 'elders' believed that the vegetable gardens were haunted on certain days of the year. No one picked vegetables on those days and so this soup was invented. They simply *had* to have their soup! This was also a popular recipe during Lent. Dried chestnuts are readily available in Portugal and can be obtained locally in shops that stock Portuguese specialities.

200 g kidney beans, soaked
   overnight
100 g dried chestnuts,
   soaked overnight
1 onion, chopped
1 stick cinnamon

60 g rice
salt to taste
10 ml olive oil
parsley
coriander leaves

Boil the beans and the chestnuts in the water in which they were soaked until they are soft. Add the rest of the ingredients, except the last two, and simmer until the rice is cooked. Sprinkle with chopped parsley or coriander leaves and serve.

**Serves 4 – 6.**

# Chicken Soup
## *Canja*

There is nothing like a good chicken soup to restore your health. By the way, did you know that this is how the name *restaurant* originated – the place where one ate a good soup? There is an old Portuguese saying that the older the bird the better the soup.

1 large chicken (about 1,2 kg
   with giblets)
2 litres water
salt

1 small onion
200 g white rice
mint leaves
lemon juice

Clean the chicken, removing all traces of blood from the cavity. This will give you a clear broth. Place the chicken in a pan with the water and add salt to taste. Add the whole onion and the giblets. Simmer until cooked – approximately 2 hours. Remove the chicken and strain the broth. Add the rice to the broth and cook until tender.

Remove the chicken meat from the bone and cut into pieces. Add to the broth. Place a sprig of mint in each soup plate and ladle the hot soup over it. Add a touch of lemon juice and 'restore' yourself.

**Serves 4 – 6.**

**Variations**
✻ Add a few slices of *chouriço* while the chicken is cooking.
✻ Spice the broth by adding a few cloves, 2 allspice, 1 stick cinnamon and 1 bayleaf.
✻ Small seed-shaped noodles may be used instead of rice.

# Meat Broth
## Caldo de Carne

500 g short ribs
25 ml butter
10 ml olive oil
1 onion, chopped
1 clove garlic, chopped
2 tomatoes, peeled and chopped
1 stick cinnamon
2 ml each ground cumin, ground
   cloves and allspice

2 litres water
2 turnips, chopped
1 carrot, chopped
potatoes (optional)
250 ml vermicelli
salt and pepper to taste
fresh thyme

Cut the meat into small pieces and fry in the butter and olive oil. Add the onion, garlic, tomatoes and spices and mix well. Simmer for 10 minutes. Add 2 litres of water and cook until the meat is tender. Add the turnips, carrot and potatoes and simmer until the vegetables are cooked. Add the vermicelli and season. When cooked, remove the meat from the soup and discard the bones. Cut the meat into small pieces and return it to the soup. Add a sprig of thyme and serve.

**Serves 4 – 6.**

## Bread Soups
### Açordas

It is a well-known fact that Portuguese housewives have developed the art of using every scrap in their larders, turning them into delicious meals (*aproveitar*). A notable example of this is most certainly the use of day-old bread which has hardened. 'Yesterday's bread' is used country-wide in many popular soups.

# Cold Tomato Soup
## Gaspacho ou Arjamolho

This is a very refreshing soup which is served on hot summer days in the Algarve. Legend has it that a farmer promised three meals a day to the men he had hired to work for him: *Arjamolho* in the morning, *Gaspacho* at lunch time, and vinegar soup in the evening. The men were very happy with this arrangement until they realised that these were three different names for the same soup . . .

3 large tomatoes, chopped
1 litre iced water
3 – 4 cloves garlic
5 ml coarse salt
20 ml olive oil

5 ml oregano
25 ml vinegar
1 green pepper, sliced
250 g day-old Portuguese
  bread
cucumber, sliced (optional)

Before starting, place the soup tureen in the refrigerator.

Liquidise 1 tomato, 250 ml iced water, the garlic, salt, oil, oregano and vinegar. Place in the tureen. Add the rest of the tomatoes, the green pepper and the rest of the water. Lastly, add the bread, cut into small cubes. Garnish with cucumber and serve immediately.

**Serves 4 – 6.**

# Pennyroyal Soup
## *Sopa de Poejos*

Pennyroyal grows abundantly, just like watercress, along riversides in Portugal. At last I have been able to grow pennyroyal successfully and I can make this delicious soup more often. There is nothing better to warm you on a winter's day.

250 ml pennyroyal
100 g bacon (spek is best)
5 – 10 ml olive oil
2 onions, chopped
1 clove garlic, crushed
salt and pepper

1 litre water
4 eggs
250 g two-day-old
  Portuguese bread
  (rolls will also do)
100 g *chouriço*, sliced

Wash the pennyroyal, removing any roots or dry leaves. If possible, use only the tips. Fry the bacon in the oil until crispy. Remove the bacon. Add the onion, garlic and pennyroyal to the oil, season with salt and pepper, and sauté until golden. Add 1 litre of water and bring to the boil. Add the eggs and poach them in the broth. Cut the bread into cubes and place in a soup tureen. Remove the eggs carefully. Pour the broth over the bread. Place the eggs, bacon and *chouriço* on top and serve immediately.

**Serves 4.**

# Bread Soup Madeira-style
## *Açorda da Madeira*

This soup is an excellent restorative on the morning after . . .

| | |
|---|---|
| 1 leek, cut lengthwise | 10 ml olive oil |
| 3 chillies, whole | salt to taste |
| 1 sprig of thyme | 2 egg yolks |
| 5 cloves garlic, whole | 4 – 6 whole eggs |

Place all the ingredients, except the eggs, in a pot. Cover with water and boil for 15 – 20 minutes. Beat the 2 egg yolks. Add 250 ml hot soup to the egg yolks and mix well. Reserve. Poach 4 – 6 whole eggs in the soup for 5 minutes. Remove the pot from the heat. Add the yolk mixture to the soup and stir.

The soup may be served with slices of bread, or as it is.

**Serves 4 – 6**, depending on how many eggs you have poached.

# Bread Soup Alentejo-style
## *Açorda Alentejana*

| | |
|---|---|
| 1 slice cod *(bacalhau)*, soaked | 1 bunch coriander |
| 1 litre water | 500 g day-old |
| salt, if necessary | Portuguese bread, |
| 50 ml olive oil | sliced |
| 5 cloves garlic | 4 – 6 eggs |

Boil the cod in the water until it is soft. (Taste the water to see if it is necessary to add any salt.) Drain, and reserve the liquid.

Meanwhile, place the oil, garlic and coriander in a soup tureen and crush into a pulp. Add the sliced bread. Poach the eggs in the *bacalhau* liquid and pour both liquid and eggs over the bread, making sure that it is completely covered. Flake the fish, removing all bones, and add to the soup just before serving. (The flaked *bacalhau* is sometimes omitted and only the fish stock is used.)

You can serve this soup as a meal on its own or as a side dish with fried or grilled fish.

**Serves 4 – 6**, depending on how many eggs you have poached.

# Seafood Bread Soup
## *Açorda de Marisco*

This soup has become very popular in recent years and is definitely a meal on its own.

500 g frozen clams in shells
500 g monkfish fillets
4 large prawns, deveined
500 g seafood mix (*marinara*)
500 g day-old Portuguese bread,
    cut into cubes

4 cloves garlic, crushed
3 – 4 whole piri piri
1 bunch fresh coriander leaves
20 ml olive oil
salt and pepper
4 eggs, beaten

Boil the clams in salted water until completely open. Drain, reserving the liquid. (Note: The liquid may be strained through a clean dish cloth.) Remove the clams from their shells, reserving a few in the shells for garnishing.

Boil the fish, whole prawns and seafood mix in salted water. Drain, but reserve the liquid.

Combine the strained liquids and simmer for 10 minutes. Place the bread cubes in a bowl and pour the hot liquid over the bread. The resulting mixture should be the consistency of thick porridge. Add some hot water if necessary.

In a large pot, fry the garlic, piri piri and coriander leaves in the olive oil. Add the bread mixture. Stir well with a wooden spoon and then add the clams, fish and seafood mix. Mix lightly and adjust the seasoning. Add the beaten eggs and stir. Remove from the heat immediately and pour into a hot earthenware dish. Garnish with the reserved clams and the whole prawns. Sprinkle with some chopped coriander leaves and serve immediately.

**Serves 4 – 6.**

# Fish and Potato Soup
## *Cozinha de Batatas e Peixe*

Today my children complain about certain of the foods served to them. Of course, there are lots of other things to eat – chips, hotdogs . . . When we were children we were not allowed to eat between meals, unless it was fruit. When mealtimes came we were hungry and anything that was presented to us was delicious – such as the following soup. If fish was not available on a particular day, eggs and *chouriço* were used instead. Even today my sister still phones me and asks me to make this soup.

3 – 4 sardines *or* 500 g rock cod
   (the head is very often used)
   *or* 250 g cockles or clams
15 ml coarse salt
15 ml olive oil
1 onion, chopped
1 clove garlic, chopped
paprika to taste

1 sprig of parsley
1 sprig of coriander
2 tomatoes, grated
1 ml saffron
5 – 6 piri piri
1 bay leaf
500 g potatoes
bread slices (optional)

Prepare the fish or seafood. If using sardines, scale, gut and salt them. Soak clams as described on p55. If using rock cod, clean, scale and salt it. Sauté the onion and garlic in the oil. Add the paprika, parsley and coriander and stir well. Add the tomatoes, saffron, piri piri and bay leaf and simmer until thick. Add the sliced potatoes and enough water to cover. Simmer for 10 minutes. If using rock cod, add it now and simmer until cooked. (If using sardines or eggs, add 5 minutes before serving. If using cockles or clams, add with the potatoes.)

   Place 2 – 3 slices of bread in each soup plate and ladle the broth over them. Once this has been eaten, serve the fish (or seafood or eggs) and potatoes.

   If you make this soup very hot you will sweat out your winter colds!

**Serves 4 – 6.**

# Fish Soups
## *Sopas de Peixe*

# Clam Soup
## *Sopa de Amêijoa*

500 g clams in shells
2 litres fish stock
100 ml white wine
1 bay leaf
2 – 3 peppercorns
1 onion, chopped
2 cloves garlic, crushed

10 ml olive oil
pepper or piri piri
125 ml grated tomato
2 ml paprika
125 ml rice
chopped coriander leaves to
   garnish

Soak the clams. Bring to the boil the stock, wine, bay leaf and peppercorns. Add the soaked clams and boil until they are all open. Strain the liquid and reserve. Remove the clams from their shells, reserving a few whole clams for garnishing.

Sauté the onion and the garlic in the olive oil. Add the pepper or piri piri, the tomato, paprika and clams. Simmer for 2 – 3 minutes. Add the strained fish stock and the rice. Bring to the boil and simmer until the rice is cooked. Adjust the seasoning and then add the whole clams and chopped coriander.

If clams are not available, use mussels.

**Serves 4 – 6.**

# Lobster Soup

## *Sopa de Lagosta*

I know what you are thinking . . . what a waste! Do remember, though, that there are places, such as the west coast, that have an abundance of lobster.

| | |
|---|---|
| 1 kg crayfish | 2 onions, chopped |
| 1 clove garlic | 4 tomatoes, grated |
| 1 bay leaf | 10 ml chopped fresh herbs |
| 1 onion | 10 ml paprika |
| 1 carrot | salt, pepper and piri piri to |
| 4 – 6 peppercorns | taste |
| 50 ml olive oil | 50 ml white wine |
| 50 g butter | 2 egg yolks |
| | 25 ml Port wine |

Remove the tail from the crayfish. Remove the shell and canal, cut the flesh into cubes and reserve.

Cover the crayfish head with water and boil with the garlic, bay leaf, onion, carrot and peppercorns for 10 – 15 minutes. Strain and reserve the liquid.

Fry the chopped onions in the olive oil and butter. Add the tomatoes, herbs, paprika, seasonings, wine and a little water. Simmer until thick. Add the raw crayfish pieces and the strained crayfish stock. Simmer until the crayfish is cooked.

Mix the egg yolks with a little water and add to the soup. Add the Port wine, bring to the boil, and serve.

**Serves 4 – 6.**

# Augusto's Tuna Fish Soup
## *Sopa de Peixe*

This is a soup typical of Madeira and in our family it tastes better if 'papa' makes it. If tuna is unavailable use any large fish such as Cape salmon or rock cod.

125 ml rice
500 g fresh or frozen fish
   (preferably with bone)
10 ml coarse salt
75 ml olive oil or cooking oil
1 onion, chopped
2 tomatoes, skinned and chopped
   (about 250 ml)
5 ml chopped parsley
garlic to taste
salt and pepper
2 potatoes, cut into small cubes
2 litres water

*Spices*
5 ml paprika
1 stick cinnamon
5 ml fish spice
1 clove
2 allspice
1 ml ground cumin

Soak the rice in 250 ml hot water. Cut the fish into cubes and sprinkle with salt.

Place the oil in a large pot. Add the onion, tomatoes, parsley, garlic and spices and 250 ml of the fish pieces. Simmer for 10 minutes, stirring occasionally. Add the drained rice, potatoes and remaining fish pieces and 2 litres of water. Simmer until the rice is completely cooked. Adjust the seasoning and serve.

This soup is delicious with hot bread and a glass of wine.

**Serves 4 – 6.**

# Fish and Seafood
## *Peixe e Marisco*

It has been said that if the sea did not exist, the

Portuguese would have invented it.

Imagine – no sea, no spices from the East, no

sizzling prawns, no grilled sardines with their

tantalising aroma, no 365 ways to cook *bacalhau*, no

*caldeirada*, no Portuguese cooking!

# Salt Cod
## *Bacalhau*

It is ironic that a nation with a love of fresh fish should have adopted the foreign salt-dried cod as its national dish. (Cod is caught in the icy waters off Newfoundland, salted at sea and brought to Portugal to dry.) There are as many recipes for cod dishes as there are days in the year – I have made a selection of the most popular ones and those that are easy to prepare.

*Bacalhau* dishes are traditionally named after the people who invented them or after the place or restaurant where they were first served. New dishes are still being created today. *Bacalhau* is so popular that a 'club' has been established in South Africa – the *Academia do Bacalhau* with branches in major South African cities and also in Portugal. Naturally, *bacalhau* dishes are served at the weekly meetings of the *Academia*.

*Bacalhau* may be bought whole or in slices. It may be stored in a grocery cupboard (but be warned of its strong smell), or well wrapped in plastic bags in the vegetable compartment of a refrigerator.

Strictly speaking, *bacalhau* should be soaked before using for 12 – 24 hours, depending on its thickness. The water should be changed 2 – 3 times during soaking. My method is somewhat different and alters the taste slightly, but it is convenient. I soak the fish for 8 – 10 hours and then place it on a tray and open-freeze it. When it is solid I pack it into freezer bags and store it in the freezer until it is required. It gets a final soak of 3 – 4 hours immediately before use.

# Brás Cod
## *Bacalhau à Brás*

This dish, invented by someone called Brás, is almost like an omelette or very fancy scrambled eggs. If you have a large crowd to feed it is best to make it in batches.

| | |
|---|---|
| 500 g *bacalhau* (well soaked) | 10 ml butter |
| 500 g potatoes | salt and pepper |
| cooking oil | chopped parsley |
| 2 onions, sliced | 6 eggs |
| 3 cloves garlic, crushed | black olives for garnishing |
| 25 ml olive oil | |

Remove the skin and bone from the fish. Cut the fish and shred it into strips. Cut the potatoes into matchsticks (or use the shredder blade of the food processor). Fry the potatoes in cooking oil until golden and soft but not crisp. Drain.

Sauté the onions and garlic in the olive oil and butter. Add the fish and fry for 4 – 5 minutes. Add half the potatoes, the seasoning and some chopped parsley. Stir lightly. Add the beaten eggs and, with the help of two egg-lifters, turn the mixture until the eggs are cooked (about 2 – 3 minutes).

To serve, place the remaining potatoes in a circle on a warmed platter. Place the fish mixture in the centre, sprinkle with chopped parsley and garnish with black olives.

**Serves 4 – 6.**

# Gomes De Sá Cod
## *Bacalhau à Gomes De Sá*

There are dozens of variations of this recipe. I will not claim that this one is the best but it is certainly delicious and easy to prepare. The use of milk to soften the cod makes it a close relative of the original recipe.

500 g *bacalhau* (preferably
    middle slices)
250 – 300 ml milk
2 large onions, sliced
2 cloves garlic, crushed
125 ml olive oil
500 g potatoes, boiled and
    thickly sliced

salt and pepper
chopped parsley
2 hard-boiled eggs, sliced or
    cut into wedges
black olives

Soak the fish overnight. Rinse and place in a saucepan. Cover with boiling water. Place the lid on the saucepan and leave to soak for about 20 minutes. Drain the fish. Remove the skin and bone and flake the fish into large flat pieces. Return the fish to the saucepan and cover it with the boiling milk. Let it stand for 1 $1/2$ – 2 hours.

In a large frying pan, fry the onions and garlic in the olive oil. Add the potatoes. Drain the fish and add it to the frying pan. Stir very gently so that the fish and potatoes do not disintegrate. Season. Transfer the mixture to an earthenware dish or casserole, drizzle with some olive oil, and bake at 200° C for 10 minutes. Remove from the oven, sprinkle with chopped parsley, and garnish with black olives and hard-boiled egg.

**Serves 4 – 6.**

**Variation**

Place a layer of potatoes in a casserole dish and add half of the fish and a third of the onions. Sprinkle with parsley. Add further layers of potato, fish and onion, ending with onion. Sprinkle with parsley and drizzle a little olive oil over the top. Bake at 180° C for 35 – 40 minutes. Garnish as above.

# Christmas Eve Cod
## *Bacalhau da Consoada ou Bacalhau com Todos*

This dish was traditionally served on Christmas Eve, after midnight mass, to break the fast. This particular meal is rapidly disappearing and the dish is now served at any meal at any time of the year. As this was one of the 'thousand dishes' to be eaten on Christmas Eve, the left-overs were useful for devising some of the 365 ways to eat cod fish.

Traditionally this dish was served with potatoes and green cabbage or broccoli and lots of garlic and olive oil. Boiled chick peas are a popular accompaniment in many restaurants *(meia desfeita de bacalhau)*. If you are catering for a large crowd, serve the different items separately.

> 1 slice *bacalhau* per person
> 2 potatoes per person
> 500 g cabbage or broccoli per person
> 1 hard-boiled egg per person

This dish is prepared just before serving. There are two ways of making it:

(1) Boil the pre-soaked fish with the cabbage or broccoli. Cook the potatoes in their jackets separately; *or*

(2) Peel the potatoes and boil them with the fish, adding the greens last.
The eggs are boiled separately for both methods.

Serve with the following sauce: In a pan, heat 75 ml olive oil per person. Add garlic to taste. Remove from the heat and *very slowly* add 5 ml wine vinegar.

# *Bacalhau* in Cream Sauce
## *Bacalhau com Natas*

500 g potatoes
cooking oil
500 g cooked and flaked
   *bacalhau*
2 onions, sliced
25 ml olive oil
100 ml grated cheese

*White sauce*
25 g butter
25 ml flour
250 ml milk
250 ml fresh cream
1 egg yolk
5 ml mustard
salt and pepper

Peel and slice the potatoes or cut into large cubes and fry in deep oil. Drain. Flake the cooked fish into large pieces. Make the white sauce (see recipe on p121), season with salt and pepper, add the mustard and 50 ml of the grated cheese.

Fry the onions in the olive oil until soft and golden. Off the heat, add the fish, the fried potatoes and the sauce. Return the pan to the heat and mix well. Cook for 5 minutes, stirring gently.

Pour into an ovenproof dish and sprinkle with the remaining cheese. Bake at 200° C until bubbly and brown – about 20 minutes.

**Serves 4 – 6.**

# João do Buraco Cod
## *Bacalhau à João do Buraco*

400 g cooked and flaked
   *bacalhau*
4 large onions, sliced
125 ml olive oil
1 tin clams without shells
250 g cooked prawns

*White sauce*
25 ml flour
25 ml butter
750 ml warm milk
2 egg yolks
50 ml chopped parsley
salt and pepper

*Mashed potatoes*
1 kg potatoes
50 g butter
milk
2 egg whites
salt and pepper

Prepare the cod (boil, remove skin and bone) and flake in large pieces. Fry the onions in the olive oil until just soft.

Make the white sauce (see recipe on p121), adding the egg yolks and parsley at the end. Season to taste.

Boil and mash the potatoes. Add the butter and enough warm milk to get a piping consistency and beat well. Season. Fold in the stiffly beaten egg whites. Place in a pastry bag fitted with a large nozzle.

Grease a deep ovenproof dish and spread a third of the onions over the bottom. Add a layer of cod, followed by a layer of clams and a layer of cooked prawns. Cover with half the white sauce. Repeat the layers, ending with onions. Cover with the remaining white sauce. Pipe the mashed potatoes over the top and brown under the grill.

**Serves 4 – 6.**

# Charcoal Grilled Cod
## *Bacalhau Assado na Brasa*

500 g *bacalhau*, soaked
  *or* 1 small whole cod fish
  (about 500 g), unsoaked
500 g new potatoes, washed

2 green peppers
vinaigrette sauce (see p122)
black olives for garnishing

Grill the whole fish over coals. Plunge immediately into cold water and leave to soak for half an hour. (Omit this step if you are using pre-soaked *bacalhau*.)

Meanwhile, boil the potatoes in their jackets and grill the green peppers.

Drain the fish on a kitchen towel. Flake and place in a bowl. Add half the vinaigrette sauce.

*To serve:* Peel the potatoes and place them on a large platter. Place the fish over the potatoes and sprinkle with strips of grilled green pepper. Pour over the remaining vinaigrette sauce and garnish with black olives.

**Serves 4.**

# Jardim's Baked Fish
## *Bacalhau à Jardim*

Oh yes, my husband has given his name to a *bacalhau* dish too!

500 g *bacalhau*, soaked
500 g small peeled potatoes
3 large tomatoes, skinned
    and chopped
2 onions, chopped
1 green pepper, chopped
1 red pepper, chopped
2 cloves garlic, crushed

5 ml chopped parsley
2 ml ground cumin
1 bay leaf
125 ml olive oil
125 ml white wine
salt and pepper
2 hard-boiled eggs
10 black olives

Cut the soaked *bacalhau* into cubes. Place together with the potatoes in a pyrex dish. Mix all the remaining ingredients *except the eggs and the olives* together in a jug and pour over the fish and potatoes. Mix well. Bake at 180° C for 40 – 45 minutes or until the fish and potatoes are cooked. Very carefully, pour the sauce into a bowl and add the chopped hard-boiled eggs and the olives. Adjust the seasoning. Pour the sauce over the fish and return to the oven for a further 10 minutes. Serve at once.
**Serves 4.**

# *Bacalhau* Pie
## *Empadão de Bacalhau*

Suitable for brunch.

750 g *bacalhau*, soaked
25 ml butter
100 ml olive oil
2 onions, chopped
2 cloves garlic, crushed
2 tomatoes, grated (about 250 ml)
2 ml freshly ground black pepper
125 ml Cheddar cheese
10 ml Parmesan cheese
125 ml breadcrumbs
2 ml ground nutmeg

*Mashed potatoes*
1 kg potatoes
salt and pepper to taste
125 ml cream
4 eggs, separated
10 ml chopped parsley

Remove the skin and bone from the soaked fish and cut into cubes. Place the oil and butter in a pan and sauté the onion and garlic for 5 minutes. Add the fish, tomatoes and black pepper and simmer for 20 minutes.

Meanwhile boil the potatoes in their jackets until tender. Peel and mash them. Season and add the cream, beaten egg yolks and parsley. Beat until fluffy.

Place the *bacalhau* mixture in a food processor and blend for 30 seconds using the chopping blade. (It is easier if done in two batches.) Mix the potato with the *bacalhau* mixture, fold in the stiffly beaten egg whites, and place in an ovenproof dish.

Mix together the cheeses, breadcrumbs and nutmeg. Sprinkle over the fish and potato mixture. Bake in a preheated oven at 180° C until golden (about 30 minutes).

**Serves 6 – 8.**

# Sardines
## *Sardinhas*

When summer comes the sweet smell of spring is transformed into the characteristic aroma of grilled sardines. Sardines are synonymous with outdoor cooking. Terracotta braziers (*fogareiros*), or two bricks, a grill and a fire, are used everywhere – on the beach or at inland picnic sites. In Portugal sardines are at their best between April and October. Unfortunately in South Africa we generally have to rely on frozen packets.

# Charcoal Grilled Sardines
## *Sardinhas Assadas*

It is difficult to give exact quantities for this dish. It is so very easy to lose track of time when eating sardines and drinking wine . . .

*For 4 people*
allow at least 5 – 6 sardines per person
250 ml coarse salt (no substitutes!)

Wash the sardines, but do not scale or gut them. Sprinkle with coarse salt and place in layers in a large bowl for 1 hour. Tilt the bowl so that the brine runs off and shake off any excess salt before grilling.

Place the sardines in a hinged grill and close the latch. Place the grill over a charcoal fire when the coals are covered with ash. Grill the sardines on both sides until they are golden (about 2 – 3 minutes per side).

Serve with boiled potatoes or potatoes baked in the cinders (Cinderella's potatoes!).

# Baked Sardines
## *Sardinhas no Forno*

This recipe combines all the Portuguese favourites in one.

| | |
|---|---|
| 12 sardines | 5 ml paprika |
| 10 ml coarse salt | salt and pepper |
| 2 large onions, sliced | 50 ml white wine |
| 2 – 3 cloves garlic, crushed | 500 g ripe tomatoes, skinned |
| 125 ml olive oil | and sliced |
| 1 red pepper, sliced | 25 ml toasted flour |
| 1 green pepper, sliced | fresh herbs (parsley, coriander |
| 1 bay leaf | leaves) |

Wash the sardines, remove the heads and gut. Sprinkle with salt.

Fry the onions and garlic in the olive oil until they are soft. Add the sliced peppers, bay leaf, paprika, salt and pepper. Simmer gently for 5 minutes. Add the wine and the sliced tomatoes. Simmer for a further 10 minutes, stirring very gently so as not to break up the ingredients.

Grease an ovenproof dish (preferably earthenware) and pour the sauce into it. Shake the excess salt from the sardines, dip them in toasted flour and arrange them on top of the sauce.

Place the dish in a very hot oven (200° C) for about 10 – 15 minutes. Remove from the oven, sprinkle with fresh chopped herbs and serve immediately.

**Serves 4 – 6.**

# Sardines from Nazaré
## *Sardinhas de Nazaré*

8 large fresh sardines
lemon juice
salt and pepper
12,5 ml flour
1 egg, beaten
breadcrumbs
oil for frying

2 tomatoes, blanched, peeled
 and chopped
25 ml olive oil
chopped spring onions to taste
chopped parsley to taste
2 hard-boiled eggs

Wash and clean the sardines. Remove head, slit from top to tail and open out flat. Remove gut and backbone. Marinate for 30 minutes in lemon juice, salt and pepper.

Dip the sardines in flour, beaten egg and breadcrumbs and fry in hot oil. Fry the tomatoes in the olive oil, adding pinches of salt and pepper, chopped spring onion and parsley.

Arrange the sardines in the shape of a fan in a round dish. Pour the tomato sauce in the centre and garnish with slices of hard-boiled egg.

**Serves 4.**

## Tuna Fish

### *Atum*

In Portugal, especially in the Algarve, and in Madeira tuna fish is eaten fresh and prepared in a variety of ways. But there is plenty left over for canning! There is a prolific tuna canning industry in the Algarve.

# Tuna Fish Steaks
## *Bifes de Atum*

There is a great dispute in my household concerning tuna fish steaks. The two recipes that follow are, respectively, from Madeira and from the Algarve. I say, of course, that my recipe is better and easier whereas my husband says that his is tastier and definitely quicker. I leave it to you to decide ...

Fresh tuna must be used. It is obtainable at most fisheries – fresh at the coast and frozen inland. Fresh tuna is dark in colour. If you would like to lighten it, soak it in cold water for 2 – 3 hours and drain it well before use.

# Madeira-style
## *Bifes de Atum da Madeira*

1 kg fresh tuna
oil for frying

*Marinade*
10 ml coarse salt
25 ml vinegar
25 ml olive oil
1 bay leaf
3 cloves garlic, crushed

1 stick cinnamon
fresh herbs (sprig each of
    parsley, thyme, oregano) *or*
5 ml dried herbs
2 allspice
5 ml paprika
5 ml ground cumin
250 ml red wine

Wash the tuna and remove the skin and bone. Slice into steaks. Mix together all the ingredients for the marinade. Pour marinade over the tuna and leave for at least 3 hours. Fry the drained tuna steaks in hot oil and then remove from the pan. Add the marinade to the pan and bring to the boil. Pour over the steaks. Serve with cooked mealie meal or fried mealie meal cubes (see p116).

**Serves 4 – 6.**

# Algarve-style
## *Bifes de Atum do Algarve*

1 kg fresh tuna
10 ml coarse salt
salt and pepper
3 large onions, sliced
garlic to taste

45 ml olive oil
250 ml white wine
1 sprig of parsley
1 bay leaf
coriander leaves

Wash the tuna and remove the skin and bone. Cut into slices and season with coarse salt. Leave for 15 minutes. Place tuna, seasoning, onion and crushed garlic in layers in a casserole. Pour over the oil and wine and add the herbs. Cover and simmer for 30 – 45 minutes. Garnish with coriander leaves. Serve with rice or potato chips.

**Serves 4 – 6.**

# Braised Tuna Fish
## *Atum Assado na Panela*

1 kg fresh tuna
3 cloves garlic, crushed
15 ml coarse salt
pepper
4 onions, sliced
2 bay leaves
250 ml red wine

15 ml vinegar
25 ml oil
25 ml butter
10 ml paprika
20 ml Madeira wine
1 sprig of thyme

Remove the skin and bone and cut the tuna into cubes. Season with garlic, salt and pepper and place in a dish. Place the sliced onions and the bay leaves on top of the tuna and pour over enough wine and vinegar to cover. A little water may be needed. Marinate for 4 hours.

Heat the oil and butter in a pan. Add the sliced onions from the marinade and sauté until soft. Add the drained tuna and cook until it is brown. Pour on the marinade and simmer until the tuna is almost cooked. Add the paprika, Madeira wine and thyme. Simmer for 5 minutes. Serve with new potatoes.

**Serves 4 – 6.**


**Variation**
Add potatoes to the pan after browning the tuna.


# Hake
## *Pescada*

Hake is also very popular in Portugal: boiled, fried, grilled or baked, it graces many tables. In Portugal small hake (about 20 centimetres long) is used whole. Hook the tail between the teeth, dip in flour and fry. A popular lunch dish is boiled hake served with potatoes, green beans or cauliflower and boiled eggs.

# Baked Hake
## *Pescada no Forno*

1 whole hake (1,25 – 1,5 kg)
lemon juice
75 ml olive oil
2 cloves garlic, crushed
salt to taste
25 ml fresh coriander leaves,
    chopped

1 chicken stock cube
2 – 3 whole piri piri
1 kg small potatoes, parboiled
    and peeled
150 ml white wine
10 ml garlic butter (see p124)

Wash and gut the hake, keeping it whole. Cut a few slits (not too deep) along the sides. Sprinkle lemon juice over the fish.

Make a paste with the olive oil, garlic, salt, coriander, stock cube and piri piri. Rub the paste over the fish and leave for 15 minutes.

Grease an ovenproof dish. Fold the fish until the tail is caught in the teeth. Place it in the dish, arrange the potatoes around the fish and pour over the wine. Dot the fish with the garlic butter and bake at 180° C for 45 minutes. Baste during cooking.

**Serves 4 – 6.**

# Stewed Hake
## *Pescada Estufada*

4 – 6 thick slices hake
juice of 1 lemon
2 cloves garlic, crushed
salt and pepper
125 ml olive oil
25 ml butter
3 onions, sliced

25 ml chopped parsley
2 ml thyme or oregano
200 ml white wine
500 ml mashed potatoes
100 ml tomato purée
10 ml flour
50 ml Port wine

Marinate the fish in the lemon juice, garlic, salt and pepper. Place half the olive oil and the butter in a large frying pan with a lid. Add half the onions. Layer the fish on top of the onions. Add the remaining onions, the parsley, thyme or oregano and white wine. Pour the rest of the oil over the fish. Cover and simmer gently for 15 minutes.

Pipe a border of mashed potato on a hot serving dish and spoon the fish into the centre. Mix the tomato purée with the flour, a little water and the Port wine. Add to the pan and simmer for 2 minutes. Adjust the seasoning and pour over the fish.

**Serves 4 – 6.**

# Fish Stew
## *Caldeirada*

*Caldeirada* is a rich fish stew, cousin to the French *bouillabaisse* and the Greek *kakavi*. This is truly a dish that boasts the richness of the Portuguese shores – the greater the variety of fish and shellfish used the tastier the stew and it is, of course, important that fresh fish be used. In some seaside restaurants in Portugal one waits for the catch of the day to be brought in and for the *caldeirada* to be freshly prepared (anyone heard of stress?). Each region has its favourite *caldeirada*, depending on the kinds of fish obtainable. Normally, four to six different kinds of fish are used. When all else fails the housewife may improvise by using salt cod, and sometimes chicken, rabbit or kid are substituted for the fish. Some recipes call for the addition of potatoes, otherwise the fish stew is served on bread.

Because of the large number and variety of ingredients it is worth while making this dish for a large number of people. It is only in recent years that my father divulged the secrets of his version of the *Caldeirada Algarvia* and, with his permission, I am sharing them with you. Thanks, *Vovô!*

# Fish Stew from the Algarve
## *Caldeirada Algarvia à Caco*

2 kg assorted fish (rock cod,
    kingklip, yellowtail, kabeljou)
500 g monkfish (a must)
25 ml coarse salt
500 g clams in shells
300 g whole prawns
10 – 12 sardines
4 large onions, sliced
1,5 kg tomatoes, sliced
3 green peppers, sliced
1,5 kg potatoes, peeled and sliced

500 g seafood mix
100 ml olive oil
250 ml white wine
3 cloves garlic, crushed
10 ml paprika
1 bay leaf
4 – 5 piri piri
coriander leaves
20 ml butter

Clean the fish and cut into serving pieces. Sprinkle with salt and leave for 30 minutes. Meanwhile, soak the clams in salted water to remove any sand. Devein the prawns. Scale and gut the sardines and remove the heads.

You will need an extra large pot for this dish. Place the clams at the bottom of the dish. They will act as a 'tripod' and prevent the stew from burning at the bottom. Place a layer of onions over the clams, followed by a layer of tomatoes, green peppers, potatoes, fish, and seafood mix. Repeat these layers. The prawns and sardines must form the top layer so that they are served first.

Mix together in a jug the olive oil, wine, crushed garlic, paprika, bay leaf and piri piri. Pour over the layers of fish and vegetables. Place the coriander leaves on top and dot with butter.

Keep the pot covered and simmer gently without stirring for about an hour. Wrap the pot in a white table cloth and place it on the table and let each guest take 'potluck'.

**Serves 10 – 12.**

# Stuffed Fish
## *Peixe Recheado*

This is my Portuguese adaptation of a great favourite.

1 whole fish – 1,5 – 2 kg (rock
    cod, kabeljou, Cape salmon)

*Stock*
fish bones
strip of lemon rind
2 cloves garlic, crushed
10 ml olive oil
5 peppercorns
1 litre water

*Stuffing*
1 onion, finely chopped
2 cloves garlic, chopped
10 ml olive oil
400 g seafood mix (separate
    packs, if available)

5 ml paprika
salt and pepper
a few sprigs of fresh herbs
200 ml fish stock
2 egg yolks
15 ml flour

*Sauce*
3 large onions, sliced
30 ml olive oil
30 ml garlic butter (see p124)
1 tomato, grated
1 bay leaf
salt and pepper
250 ml fish stock
250 ml white wine
15 ml chopped fresh herbs

Cut the fish open and remove the middle bone carefully. Place the bone and all the ingredients for the stock in a saucepan and simmer for 1 hour. Strain.

Meanwhile, prepare the stuffing. Sauté the chopped onion and garlic in the olive oil. Add the seafood mix, stir, and then add the paprika, seasoning, herbs, and a little stock. Simmer for 5 minutes. Mix together the egg yolks, flour and the rest of the stock. Add to the pan and stir until thick.

Season the fish with salt and pepper. Place the stuffing in the middle of the fish and tie with string. Place in an ovenproof dish.

Now prepare the sauce. Sauté the onions in the oil and butter. Add the tomato and bay leaf and season with salt and pepper. Add the stock, white wine and herbs and simmer for 2 – 3 minutes. Pour the sauce over the fish and bake in a preheated oven at 180° C for 40 – 45 minutes.

Serve with parsley potatoes.

**Serves 6 – 8.**

# Grilled or Fried Fish
## *Peixe Assado ou Frito*

The best dishes are often the easiest to prepare. Because fish is abundant and Portuguese people must have two main meals a day, lunch is often a quick dish of charcoal-grilled or fried fish served with a lettuce salad. Fish such as red roman, mackerel, small rock cod, small kabeljou and haarders are suitable.

Clean the fish, gut and scale and score the sides. Sprinkle with salt and leave for 30 minutes. Shake off the salt. Brush with olive oil. Grill over moderate coals, basting continuously with olive oil. Serve with a vinaigrette sauce (see p122).

To fry fish, clean and prepare as described above. Dip into seasoned flour. Shallow-fry in a mixture of two-thirds cooking oil to one-third olive oil. Drain and serve.

# Fish in Batter
## *Peixe em Capote*

500 g fish fillet, cut into
    strips and marinated for
    1 hour
oil for deep-frying

*Marinade*
10 ml salt
2 ml pepper
5 ml lemon pepper
25 ml oil
2 cloves garlic, crushed
15 ml lemon juice
1 sprig of parsley

*Batter*
250 g flour
2 eggs, separated
1 egg white
50 ml olive oil *or* 25 ml olive oil
    and 25 ml cooking oil
75 ml beer
salt and pepper
100 ml water (approximately)

*Clockwise from the left*
Kale Soup; *Chouriço*; Mealie Meal Bread

*Clockwise from the left*
Prawn Patties; Grilled Portuguese Sausage; Savoury Carrots;
Cod Fish Cakes; Pickled Octopus; Lupins; Pickled Tuna;
Chicken Livers; Portuguese Rolls

Sift the flour, add the egg yolks, oil, beer, salt, pepper and enough water to make a soft batter. Beat well. Rest for 1 hour. Just before frying the fish, beat the 3 egg whites and fold into the batter. Drain the marinated fish, dip it into the batter and fry in deep oil. Drain on paper.

**Serves 4 – 6.**

# Fish Salad
## *Salada de Peixe*

1 tin tuna fish
250 g cooked prawns, halved
250 g cooked peas
250 g cooked carrots, diced
3 potatoes, boiled and cut
   into cubes
375 ml mayonnaise

2 ml curry powder
salt and pepper to taste
lettuce
1 hard-boiled egg
olives for garnishing
chopped parsley

Mix the tuna, the prawns and the vegetables in a large bowl. Add the mayonnaise, curry powder and seasonings. Toss lightly.

Serve on a bed of lettuce, or on a fish-shaped platter. Garnish with egg yolk, olives and chopped parsley.

This salad is suitable as a starter, served in individual fish-shaped dishes. Garnish with strips of egg white, chopped parsley and sieved egg yolk arranged in bands to resemble a fish. Place an olive for the eye and half-slices of lemon for the fins and tail.

**Serves 4 – 6.**

# Swordfish (or Scabbard fish) with Olives

## *Espada Frita com Azeitonas*

*Espada* (swordfish or scabbard fish) is a very popular fish for frying or grilling. It may be obtained frozen from most fisheries. The silver variety is imported from Portugal and the black variety from Madeira.

To prepare *espada* rub off the black skin before cooking, cut into slices diagonally and fry or grill. In Madeira *espada* is often served with bananas.

| | |
|---|---|
| 500 g *espada* | *Marinade* |
| 125 ml seasoned flour | 75 ml olive oil |
| 12 black olives | 3 cloves garlic, whole |
| 100 ml white wine | 10 ml lemon juice |
| 25 ml Madeira wine | 5 ml fresh herbs (parsley thyme) |
| oil for frying | salt and pepper |

Combine all the ingredients for the marinade and pour over the fish. Leave for 1 – 2 hours, and then drain on paper towel. Dip the fish in the flour and shallow-fry. Add the olives, wines and marinade to the pan and simmer for a few seconds.

Alternatively, the fish may be grilled and the marinade, wines and olives boiled together and then poured over the fish.

**Serves 4 – 6.**

# Squid

## *Lulas*

Was it the Portuguese who upgraded the squid (*lulas*) from fishing bait to gourmet dish?

Squid is obtained mostly in frozen form, either whole or as ready-to-use sacs, rings and even steaks. Whole squid should be prepared in the following way. Working under running water, grasp the head firmly with one hand and the body section with the other and pull gently until the head and entrails come away from the body sac. Cut the tentacles from the head, and discard the rest of the head and the entrails. Rub off the skin on the sac, turn inside out and wash again.

# Stuffed Squid
## *Lulas Recheadas*

This is my grandfather's version of a great recipe. I remember as a child helping to fill the little sacs and using oregano sticks to secure the stuffing. It is a time-consuming recipe, but well worth while. Choose medium-sized squid. Ready clean sacs may be used, but the tentacles and side wings make a very tasty filling.

12 medium-sized squid

*Stuffing*
125 g rindless bacon
10 ml olive oil
1 onion, finely chopped
1 clove garlic, crushed
squid tentacles and side wings,
   chopped
125 ml grated tomato
20 ml white wine
salt and pepper
5 ml chopped parsley
100 ml rice or very small noodles

*Sauce*
2 onions, chopped
2 cloves garlic, chopped
25 ml olive oil
1 green pepper, cut into strips
500 ml grated tomato
1 bay leaf
5 ml paprika
black pepper
salt

Clean the squid as described above. Reserve the sacs. Chop the side wings and tentacles very finely. Prepare the stuffing first and while it is cooking prepare the sauce in which the squid are to be cooked.

*To make the stuffing:* Chop the bacon very finely and fry in the olive oil until crisp. Add the onion and garlic and sauté for 5 minutes. Add the chopped tentacles and side wings, the tomato, wine, seasoning, parsley and rice or pasta. Simmer for 10 – 15 minutes.

*To prepare the sauce:* Using a deep frying pan with a lid, fry the onions and garlic in the olive oil. Add the green pepper, tomato, bay leaf, paprika and black pepper. Simmer for 10 – 15 minutes.

*To stuff the squid:* Using a small teaspoon, place stuffing in the sac until it is three-quarters full. Secure the top of the sac with a toothpick. Do not overfill the sac. There must be enough room for the stuffing to expand during cooking – otherwise the sac will burst. Place the squid in the sauce (any left-over stuffing may be added to the sauce) and simmer gently for 40 – 45 minutes. Remove the toothpicks and add salt just before serving.

This dish is usually served with plain rice and lots of red wine.

**Serves 4 – 6.**

**Variations for the stuffing**

∗ Use *chouriço* instead of bacon.

∗ Use chopped prawns or clams instead of squid tentacles.

∗ If you are feeling extravagant, use the whole lot – *chouriço*, tentacles, prawns and clams. Don't be surprised if you spend the rest of your life stuffing squid!

# Stewed Squid
## *Caldeirada de Lulas*

Portuguese housewives are very fond of the pressure cooker. This is a recipe especially for pressure cooker owners. It takes 5 minutes to cook.

| | |
|---|---|
| 1 kg squid | 1 bay leaf |
| 25 ml olive oil | 10 ml paprika |
| 2 onions, sliced | 3 whole piri piri (optional) |
| 2 cloves garlic, crushed | 100 ml white wine |
| 1 kg potatoes, each cut into | 5 ml vinegar |
| 4 pieces | salt to taste |
| 10 ml butter or margarine | 2 ml ground nutmeg |
| 5 ripe tomatoes, grated | 2 sprigs of parsley |

Clean the squid and cut into rings. Sauté the onions in the olive oil and add the garlic. Add the squid and the remaining ingredients. If using a pressure cooker, close the lid. As soon as pressure is reached, lower the temperature and leave for 5 minutes. Place the pressure cooker under running water before opening.

If you do not have a pressure cooker, place the ingredients in layers in a large pot. Start with a layer of onions and garlic, followed by a layer of potatoes, squid and tomatoes. Finish with a layer of onions. Mix all the remaining ingredients in a jug and pour over. Cover and simmer over medium heat for 20 – 25 minutes.

**Serves 4 – 6.**

# Squid au Gratin
## *Lulas Gratinadas*

1 kg squid
50 ml olive oil
1 large onion, chopped
2 cloves garlic, crushed
100 ml white wine
bouquet garni (bay leaf,
   parsley, celery)
80 ml tomato purée
salt and pepper
25 ml Port wine

*White sauce*
50 g butter or margarine
60 g flour
500 ml milk
5 ml curry powder (optional)
2,5 ml mustard
2,5 ml paprika
250 ml grated cheese

Clean the squid as described on p46. Cut the body into rings. Cut the wing flesh and tentacles into small pieces.

Fry the onion and garlic in the olive oil. Add the squid, wine, bouquet garni, tomato purée and seasoning. Simmer gently for 15 minutes. Check the seasoning. Add the Port wine.

Make the white sauce, following the recipe given on p121. Add the curry powder, mustard, paprika and 125 ml of the grated cheese.

Add two-thirds of the white sauce to the squid and pour into an ovenproof dish. Spread the remaining sauce over the top and sprinkle with the rest of the grated cheese. Bake in a hot oven (200° C) until brown.

**Serves 4 – 6.**

**Variation**
Substitute 500 ml cooked rice for the white sauce. Add the rice to the squid, mix well, and pour into a greased ovenproof dish. Beat 2 eggs and pour carefully over the squid and rice mixture. Bake at 180° C until the egg has set.

# Cuttlefish with Ink
## *Chocos com Tinta*

Cuttlefish (*chocos*) are similar to squid but the body is slightly rounder and contains a small sac with the 'ink' that gives the dish extra flavour (and your teeth extra colour). It also contains a shell or cuttlebone.

I dare you to try this recipe . . . or did you think that cuttlefish was for canaries only?

Clean the cuttlefish under running water to remove any sand, but be very careful not to burst the ink sac. Remove the 'eyes' and the inner cuttlebone.

| | |
|---|---|
| 150 ml olive oil | 5 ml paprika |
| 8 – 10 cloves garlic, crushed | 1 kg small cuttlefish |
| piri piri to taste | salt and pepper |
| 1 bay leaf | |

Use a large frying pan with a lid. Heat the oil and add the garlic, piri piri, bay leaf and paprika. Remove from the heat immediately. Add the cuttlefish. Cover the pan and simmer until the cuttlefish are tender, stirring from time to time. Season with salt and pepper.

The cooking time depends on the size of the cuttlefish. Do not overcook as this will toughen the cuttlefish.

Serve with lemon wedges and lots of home-made bread.

**Serves 4 – 6**.

## Other Seafood Dishes

# Seafood in a *Cataplana*
## *Cataplana de Marisco*

A *cataplana* is a hinged metal dish shaped like a giant clam shell (rather like a wok with a lid). They are very beautiful. I have a copper one which I keep as an ornament and an aluminium one for cooking. The lid closes with a clamp so that the steam and juices are sealed inside. In the absence of a *cataplana* use a saucepan with a very tightly fitting lid. The *cataplana* is used mainly for seafood dishes or for combinations of seafood and meat dishes.

250 g clams in shells
750 g monkfish
10 ml coarse salt
500 g langoustines or prawns
100 ml olive oil
2 onions, sliced
2 cloves garlic, crushed
1 bay leaf

75 g *chouriço*, sliced
1 tomato, grated
piri piri to taste
2 green peppers, cut into strips
2 red peppers, cut into strips
1 sprig of coriander leaves
125 ml white wine
75 ml Port wine

Soak the clams in salted water to remove any sand. Cut the monkfish into cubes and sprinkle with coarse salt. Devein the prawns.

Place 75 ml olive oil in a small saucepan. Add the onion rings, garlic and bay leaf and sauté for a few minutes. Add the *chouriço,* tomato and piri piri.

Pour the remaining 25 ml olive oil into the *cataplana* and layer the fish, clams and langoustines in it. Pour over the tomato mixture and cover with pepper strips. Place the coriander on top. Pour over the wines. Cover and cook for 20 minutes. The *cataplana* should only be opened at the table.

**Serves 4 – 6.**

# Grilled Prawns
## *Camarão Grelhado*

24 prawns
15 ml lemon juice
10 ml salt
5 – 6 whole piri piri
4 cloves garlic, crushed
25 ml olive oil

*Garlic sauce*
125 ml butter
2 cloves garlic, whole or chopped
3 whole piri piri
1 bay leaf
25 ml lemon juice

Slit the back of each prawn and remove the vein. Make a paste with the remaining ingredients. Press the paste into the cut along the back of each prawn and close. Sprinkle any remaining paste over the prawns and marinate for 2 – 3 hours. Grill the prawns over moderate coals, basting continuously with the marinade. Serve with garlic sauce.

To make the garlic sauce, melt the butter in a small saucepan, add the garlic, piri piri and bay leaf and bring to the boil. Remove from the heat, add the lemon juice and mix well.

Alternatively, prawns may be shallow-fried.

**Serves 4 – 6.**

# Prawns in Beer Sauce
## *Camarão no Forno*

1 kg prawns
25 ml lemon juice
10 ml salt
75 ml butter

75 ml olive oil
5 cloves garlic, crushed
piri piri to taste
500 ml beer

Devein the prawns, and marinate in lemon juice and salt for 10 minutes. Place in a roasting pan. Melt the butter in a saucepan, add the olive oil, garlic, piri piri and beer. Pour over the prawns and leave for 10 minutes. Bake at 180° C for 15 – 20 minutes.

It may not be traditional, but try adding a little cream to the sauce . . .
**Serves 4 – 6.**

# Prawns Zambezia
## *Camarões à Zambezia*

This was a speciality of the Zambezia province in Mozambique. This province was celebrated for its great coconut groves and the lavish entertaining of the Portuguese population. If you had the honour to be invited to one of their mansions you would more than likely be presented with a meal of 30 – 40 dishes.

4 medium brinjals
salt
20 ml seasoned flour
2 eggs, beaten
cooking oil
1 onion, chopped
15 ml olive oil

1 small tomato, grated
1 bay leaf
piri piri to taste
125 ml coconut milk (see p125)
500 g prawns (or more if you like)
breadcrumbs
ground nutmeg

Slice the brinjals. Sprinkle with salt and leave for 15 minutes. Rinse and dry on kitchen towel. Dip into seasoned flour and beaten egg and fry in cooking oil.

Fry the onion in the olive oil, add the tomato, bay leaf and piri piri to taste. Simmer for 1 – 2 minutes. Add the coconut milk. Check the seasoning and then add the deveined prawns.

Layer the brinjals and prawns in an ovenproof dish. Sprinkle breadcrumbs and nutmeg over the top and bake in a moderate oven (175° C) for 15 – 20 minutes. Serve with white rice.
**Serves 4 – 6.**

# Grilled Lobster (Crayfish)
## *Lagosta Grelhada*

20 ml Port wine
1 bay leaf
1 sprig of parsley
4 lobsters (approximately
   300 – 500 g each)
20 ml butter
2 cloves garlic, crushed
5 ml salt
3 peppercorns or ground black
   pepper

*Sauce*
250 g butter
2 cloves garlic, crushed
4 egg yolks
5 ml garlic vinegar
5 ml lemon juice

Pour the wine into a glass, add the bay leaf and parsley and leave for 30 minutes.

Live lobsters must be used. (Let the fishmonger kill them for you.) Cut each lobster in half. Remove the canal and clean. Remove the legs. Make a paste with the butter, garlic, salt, pepper and flavoured Port wine (remove the bay leaf and parsley). Rub the lobsters with the paste and leave for 10 – 15 minutes.

Meanwhile boil the lobster legs in salt water. (Offer some to your guests if they arrive early.)

Grill the lobster for about 5 minutes, flesh side downwards, turn and grill for a further 10 – 15 minutes, depending on size. The lobster is ready when the shell is bright red. Serve with the sauce.

To make the sauce, melt the butter, add the garlic and cook for 1 minute. Remove the garlic if you wish. Whisk the egg yolks in a bowl, and slowly add the melted butter. Return the mixture to the saucepan. Cook very slowly, stirring all the time, until the mixture is thick. Remove from the heat. Add the vinegar, lemon juice and some of the flesh from the lobster legs.

**Serves 4.**

# Crab Curry
## *Caril de Caranguejo*

2 kg crab
coarse salt
25 ml olive oil
10 ml cooking oil
2 onions, chopped
5 cloves garlic, crushed
1 sprig of curry leaves
1 bay leaf
5 ml ground cumin
5 ml turmeric

5 ml ground coriander
2 – 3 cloves
1 stick cinnamon
2 – 3 cardamom seeds
4 tomatoes, grated
500 ml beer
250 ml coconut milk (see p125)
25 ml curry powder
25 ml flour
fresh coriander leaves

Clean the crab. Keep all the edible pieces (legs, claws). Discard the spongy matter from the shell but keep the flesh. Wash several times and sprinkle with salt.

Heat the oils in a large pan. Add the onions and garlic and sauté until soft. Add the curry leaves, bay leaf and the rest of the spices. Stir well. Add the grated tomatoes and beer and cook until the mixture resembles a thick gravy. Add the crab and stir. Cover and cook for about 20 minutes.

Mix the coconut milk, curry powder and flour in a bowl. Add a little hot gravy to the bowl, mix well and pour into the pan. Add the chopped coriander leaves and bring to the boil. Simmer for 5 – 10 minutes.

This dish should be made at least 8 – 10 hours before serving.

**Serves 4 – 6.**

# Clams in Coriander Sauce
## *Amêijoa de Coentrada*

1,5 kg clams in shells
100 ml olive oil
10 ml garlic butter (see p124)
4 cloves garlic, crushed

2 – 3 whole piri piri
bunch of coriander leaves
25 ml lemon juice

Soak the clams in salted water for at least 4 hours. Wash several times, using fresh water each time.

Heat the olive oil and the garlic butter. Add the garlic and piri piri and fry until soft. Add the clams and coriander leaves. Check the seasoning and add a little salt if necessary. Cover the pan and simmer until all the clams have opened, stirring from time to time. Add the lemon juice and serve.

**Serves 4.**

**Variation**
Add 1 chopped onion, 2 chopped tomatoes and 5 ml paprika to the oil and cook for 5 minutes. Then proceed as above.

# Grilled Limpets
## *Lapas Grelhadas*

Limpets are a protected species and only a limited number may be harvested each year. Contact your local department of environmental affairs for details.

In Madeira special frying pans are available for grilling limpets. The base of the pan has grooves to hold the limpet shells so that the delicious sauce is not lost during grilling.

Wash limpets and soak them in salt water for 2 – 3 hours. Rinse and place, shell down, on a grill. Choose a grill that has bars going both ways, so that the shells balance in the squares. (You can play noughts and crosses with them.) Place approximately 2 ml butter on each limpet. Cook over coals or under a grill for 2 – 3 minutes. Squeeze lemon juice over each limpet and serve with lots of fresh bread and lots of wine.

# Meats
## *Carnes*

Before the days of supermarkets, and before fridges,
freezers and other modern commodities
invaded Portuguese homes, housewives in the
countryside made use of whatever they
produced on their farms. Chicken, rabbit, kid and
pork were often used. In the cities, housewives
visited their local markets every day (how else could
they keep up with the gossip?) and cooked for their
families whatever was in season, fresh and
reasonably priced. Today, most people do their
shopping once a week, but whenever possible
meat and vegetables are still bought on a daily basis.
Beef was, and still is, used mainly as steaks –
it is amazing how one carcass can yield so many
steaks. *Um bifinho* ('a little steak') is a common
expression at the butchery. *Bife* or *bifa* is a term
which also refers to an English person – perhaps
because of the 'beefeaters'?

# Beef and Veal
## *Carne de Vaca e Vitela*

# *Prego* Rolls
## *Pregos*

*Prego* rolls are made with beef but *bifana* rolls are made with pork. Whichever kind of meat you decide to place inside a Portuguese roll, once you have tasted it you are hooked.

| | |
|---|---|
| 500 – 600 g rump steak, Scotch fillet *or* topside | **Marinade** |
| | 4 – 6 cloves garlic, pressed |
| 20 ml olive oil | salt to taste |
| 20 g butter | 125 ml white wine |
| 1 bay leaf | piri piri to taste |
| 4 Portuguese rolls, buttered | pinch of ground cumin |

Slice the meat thinly. Mix together all the ingredients for the marinade and place the meat in it for 3 – 4 hours. Heat the oil, butter and bay leaf in a pan. Fry the steaks to taste. Add the marinade to the pan and simmer until thick.

Cut open the Portuguese rolls and dip the inside of each roll into the gravy. Place the steak in the roll and eat it at once. Or place the steak on the roll, spoon the gravy carefully over it and close the roll to absorb the gravy.
**Serves 4.**

# Rump Steak and Eggs
## *Bifes à Cavalo*

Traditionally this meal is prepared and served in individual earthenware dishes.

| | |
|---|---|
| 4 rump steaks | 2 bay leaves |
| 5 cloves garlic, crushed | salt and pepper |
| 15 ml olive oil | 5 ml piri piri sauce |
| 25 ml butter | 4 fried eggs |

Rub each steak with crushed garlic and leave for 30 minutes. Heat the olive oil in a frying pan and add the butter and bay leaves. Fry each steak, according to taste, on both sides. Season with salt and pepper and place on a warm plate.

Add the piri piri sauce to the pan, bring to the boil and pour over the steaks. Serve with a fried egg on top of each steak, surrounded by potato chips.
**Serves 4.**

**Variation**
Add 125 ml cream and 5 ml prepared mustard to the juices in the pan. Bring to the boil, add 25 ml Port wine and pour over the steak. (You may omit the fried egg if you wish.)

# Steak with Onions
## *Bifes de Cebolada*

Another of my father's favourite recipes. It is delicious made in an earthenware casserole.

| | |
|---|---|
| 500 g Scotch fillet *or* rump steak | 3 large onions, sliced |
| 3 cloves garlic, crushed | 1 sprig of parsley |
| piri piri to taste | 1 bay leaf |
| 20 ml olive oil | 5 ml salt |
| 20 ml butter | 100 ml white wine |

Cut the steak into thin slices and rub with the garlic and piri piri. Fry lightly in the oil and butter. Place a layer of onions in a flameproof casserole and cover with a layer of steak. Repeat the layers. Place the parsley and bay leaf on top. Dissolve the salt in the wine and pour over the steak and onion layers. Simmer for 20 minutes.
**Serves 4 – 6.**

**Variation**
Tomato slices may be added between the layers of onion and steak.

# My Mother's Favourite Steaks
## *Bifes Enrolados*

This recipe takes care of the tougher steak cuts. It really was a treat when my mother made this dish.

| | |
|---|---|
| 6 thin slices of topside | 30 ml olive oil |
| salt, pepper, garlic and piri piri to taste | 15 ml butter |
| | 125 ml wine |
| 6 hard-boiled eggs, shelled | 10 ml paprika |
| 2 carrots, boiled | 1 sprig of parsley or thyme |
| 1 *chouriço* | 75 ml tomato purée |

Place the slices of topside on a board. Season with salt, pepper, garlic and piri piri. Cut the carrots and the *chouriço* into 6 strips. Place an egg in the centre of each slice of meat and arrange a strip of carrot on one side of the egg and a strip of *chouriço* on the other. Roll the meat slices and tie with string. Heat the oil and the butter in a pan, add the steaks and brown. Add the wine, paprika, herbs and tomato purée. Simmer for 30 – 40 minutes. Remove the string and serve whole or sliced.

**Serves 6.**

# Kebabs on Bay Tree Sticks
## *Espetada à Madeirense*

To save time while working in the fields, or at large church gatherings *(festas)*, it is the custom in Madeira to skewer chunks of beef on bay sticks and to grill them over glowing coals. In restaurants today kebabs are served on iron skewers which hang from a rack.

This is a very easy recipe to try at home and it is amazing what an atmosphere it creates. The host offers the bay stick skewers to guests, who help themselves to chunks of meat. (Don't forget to leave a hand free for the wine.) If you are using iron skewers, throw a few dried bay leaves into the fire – they produce a wonderful aroma. Use fillet steak if you are grilling the kebabs in the oven, or rump steak if you are braaiing.

| | |
|---|---|
| 1 kg rump steak *or* Scotch fillet | 10 ml coarse salt |
| 3 – 4 cloves garlic, crushed | 10 ml black pepper |
| 2 bay leaves, crushed | garlic or herb butter (see p124) |

*Clockwise from the left*
Grilled Prawns; Assorted Seafood in a *Cataplana*; Stuffed Squid

*Clockwise from the left*
Lettuce Salad; Stone Bread; Piri Piri Chicken;
Pork with Clams Portuguese-style; Kebabs on Bay Tree Sticks

Cut the meat into cubes. Place in a bowl and season with the garlic, bay leaves, coarse salt and pepper. Leave for 5 – 10 minutes. Thread the cubes of meat on to sticks or skewers. Grill or braai for 5 – 10 minutes on each side. Brush with melted butter and serve on the stick or skewer. It is easy to remove the meat from the stick or skewer with the aid of a chunk of buttered bread.

**Serves 6 – 8.**

# Beef Casserole
## *Carne no Forno*

This is one of those 'my-mother-can-do-it-better' recipes. My husband has fond childhood memories of the way this dish was prepared on Christmas Eve. It was made in a huge iron pot which was placed in the clay oven after the bread and cakes had been baked. It was cooked all night, ready for the first meal on Christmas Day.

| | |
|---|---|
| 2 kg wing rib, cut into cubes | 4 ripe tomatoes, cubed |
| 1 kg small potatoes | 1 bay leaf |
| 3 chou-chou | 10 ml paprika |
| 3 sliced carrots | salt and white pepper to taste |
| 10 – 15 olives | 5 ml ground cumin |
| ground nutmeg | 3 allspice |
| | 2 cloves |
| *Marinade* | 1 stick cinnamon |
| 3 onions, chopped | 1 sprig of fresh thyme |
| 25 ml oil | 500 ml red wine |
| 2 cloves garlic, crushed | |

Place the meat and all the ingredients for the marinade in a large iron casserole. Mix well and leave for 3 – 4 hours. Add the vegetables and olives and sprinkle with nutmeg. Cover and cook overnight in a very slow oven, or at 160° C for 1 1/2 – 2 hours.

**Serves 6 – 8.**

# Pot Roast
## *Carne Estufada*

200 g bacon or spek
1,5 kg topside
30 ml olive oil
15 ml cooking oil
3 onions, chopped
2 cloves garlic, crushed

1 sprig of parsley
10 ml paprika
2 bay leaves
1 tomato, grated
250 ml red wine

Cut the bacon into strips and with the aid of a wooden skewer pierce holes in the topside and fill with the bacon (pieces of carrot and *chouriço* can also be used). Place the oils in a pot. Brown the meat on all sides and then add the onions, garlic, parsley, paprika, bay leaves, tomato and half the red wine. Simmer gently for about 1 hour, adding the rest of the wine when necessary. Serve with small potatoes fried in cooking oil.

**Serves 6 – 8.**

# Veal Spit Roast
## *Vitela no Espeto*

1 kg boneless leg of veal
salt and piri piri to taste
25 ml olive oil

10 ml wine vinegar
1 bay leaf
3 cloves garlic, crushed

Sprinkle the meat with a little salt and piri piri. Tie the veal leg into a roll. Make a paste with the remaining ingredients and rub all over the meat. Place the meat on a spit and grill or braai over medium coals, turning often. Place the left-over paste in an ovenproof dish and keep it close to the heat. Using a pastry brush or a bunch of parsley, baste the meat often with the left-over paste.

A 'butterfly' leg may be used instead of rolling the meat. This should be braaied flat.

**Serves 4 – 6.**

# Stuffed Fillets of Veal
## *Filete de Vitela Recheado*

1 kg veal fillet
2 cloves garlic, pressed or
   finely chopped
salt and pepper
6 thick slices *presunto*
50 ml white wine

50 ml olive oil
pinch of thyme or marjoram
10 ml lemon juice
10 – 12 small onions
1 tot Madeira or Port wine

Cut the fillet into thick slices, but do not cut right through – keep it whole. Rub the meat well with the garlic, salt and pepper. Insert a slice of *presunto* into each slit in the fillet. Place the meat in a roasting dish. Mix together the white wine, oil, herbs and lemon juice and pour over the meat. Add the onions. Place in an oven preheated to 180° C and roast for 30 – 40 minutes. Warm the Madeira or Port wine in a small saucepan and ignite it. Pour the flaming wine over the veal and serve.

   **Serves 4 – 6.**

**Variations**

✳ Keep the fillet whole. Cut a deep pocket lengthwise in the fillet. Make a paste of the garlic, salt, pepper and minced *presunto* and fill the pocket with the paste. Tie with string, and then proceed as above.

✳ Cut the fillet into thick slices. Cut a pocket in the centre of each slice and insert a slice of *presunto*. Secure with a toothpick. Season with garlic, salt and pepper. Dip twice into beaten egg and breadcrumbs and fry.

# Pork
## *Porco*

# Pork and Bean Stew
## *Feijoada*

Each region of Portugal has its own speciality, usually dictated by the ingredients available in its 'larder'. This recipe is not to be confused with its sister *Feijoada Brasileira*, which uses black beans. In many places this dish is made to use up pigs' ears, trotters and heads, but I have used more acceptable pork cuts. Try it.

| | |
|---|---|
| 500 g kidney, butter or sugar<br>   beans, soaked overnight | 10 ml cooking oil |
| | 15 ml olive oil |
| 1 pork knuckle, salted overnight | 2 onions, chopped |
| 1 small piece each of *chouriço*<br>   and blood sausage | 5 cloves garlic, crushed |
| | 250 g pork belly, cut into pieces |
| 1 small onion | 250 g pork rib, cut into pieces |
| 1 carrot | 1 pork sausage |
| 10 ml olive oil | 1 blood sausage |
| 1 bay leaf | 2 tomatoes, grated |
| 2 cloves | 25 ml chopped parsley |
| 5 peppercorns | salt, pepper and piri piri |
| | 10 ml paprika |

Drain the beans, place in a large saucepan and cover with water. Add the pork knuckle, pieces of *chouriço* and blood sausage, the onion, carrot, 10 ml olive oil, bay leaf, cloves and peppercorns and boil until almost tender. Drain, and reserve the stock.

In a heavy pot, heat the 10 ml cooking oil and 15 ml olive oil and fry the chopped onion and crushed garlic. Add the pork belly and ribs and fry gently over a low heat for 15 – 20 minutes. Add the thickly sliced pork and blood sausages, the tomatoes and 250 ml stock from the beans. Simmer until the meat is tender. Add the beans and chopped parsley and adjust the seasoning. Add more stock if necessary. Cook for a further 10 minutes so that the flavours mingle.

Serve with rice garnished with carrot and some of the sausage slices. In some regions broccoli is added just before serving.

**Serves 4 – 6.**

*Feijoada Brasileira* is a stew made of pork (trotters, ears and tail), beef, smoked tongue, dried meat (almost like biltong), different sausages and, of course, black beans. Kassler rib and spare ribs are good substitutes. It is served with white rice, sliced oranges and manioc flour or *farofa*.

# Pork with Clams Portuguese-style
## *Carne de Porco com Amêijoas à Portuguesa*

We have been nicknamed 'Pork and Cheese' – I am sure this should have been 'Pork and Clams'. It has been said (I am open to correction) that during the sixteenth century the Portuguese made up dishes of pork and shellfish in order to test people's religions. No matter how it all started, it is a most successful combination. A delicious example is the very popular recipe that follows.

1 kg pork loin, cut into cubes
20 ml olive oil
25 ml lard
50 ml olive oil   } for frying
1 small onion, chopped
3 tomatoes, grated
25 ml chopped parsley
salt and pepper
1,5 kg clams (soaked as
   described on p55)

*Marinade*
50 g red pepper paste (see p194)
   *or* 10 ml paprika
5 peppercorns
2 bay leaves
200 ml white wine
5 – 6 cloves garlic, crushed
2 cloves
salt

Mix together the ingredients for the marinade, add the pork cubes and leave for 2 – 3 hours. Drain the pork and reserve the marinade. Heat the 20 ml olive oil and the lard in a large frying pan. Fry the pork until brown. Add the marinade and simmer for 10 – 15 minutes until tender.

Meanwhile, heat the 50 ml olive oil in a saucepan. Add the onion, tomatoes and parsley. Season. Cook for 4 – 5 minutes. Add the clams. Cover and cook until the clams open – about 20 minutes. Add the clams and their sauce to the pork and reheat.

Serve with cubed fried potatoes and lots of red wine.

**Serves 4 – 6.**

**Variation**
Add the washed clams to the pork, stir well, cover and cook for 30 minutes.

# Pork Schnitzel
## *Febras de Porco*

This dish is typical of the Minho region.

750 g pork schnitzels

**Marinade**
6 cloves garlic, crushed
salt and pepper
1 bay leaf

2 ml ground cumin
5 ml vinegar
125 ml white wine
5 ml paprika
sprig of fresh herbs

Mix together the ingredients for the marinade and pour over the schnitzels. Leave for a couple of hours and then drain and fry or grill.

Serve with parboiled potatoes, cut into thick slices and fried.

**Serves 4.**

# Crispy Pork with Chestnuts
## *Rojões*

1 kg pork loin, cut into cubes
100 g pork liver (optional)
20 ml oil
25 ml lard
1,5 kg boiled chestnuts
orange and lemon slices
black olives

**Marinade**
350 ml white wine
2 cloves garlic, crushed
10 ml paprika
1 bay leaf
2 cloves
5 ml cumin seeds
salt and pepper to taste

Mix together the ingredients for the marinade, pour over the meat and leave for at least a day. Drain, and reserve the marinade. Fry the meat in a mixture of the oil and lard. Add half the marinade and simmer until tender. Fry the liver and add to the pork. Fry the chestnuts and add to the pan. Add the remaining marinade and simmer until the chestnuts are tender.

Garnish with orange and lemon slices and black olives.

**Serves 4.**

# Pork in Wine and Garlic Sauce
## *Carne de Vinha d'Alhos ou*
## *Carne de Vinho e Alhos*

Madeira is one of those places where Christmas traditions are so closely adhered to that one really looks forward to the *festa*. Cooking preparations start months in advance. It is at this time of year that the prize pig is slaughtered so that there is enough pork for a Christmas lunch of *Vinha d'Alhos*.

1 kg pork loin
20 ml lard
25 ml oil
5 slices bread
orange slices

**Vinha d'alhos marinade**
200 ml white wine
200 ml vinegar

1 tot Madeira wine
3 cloves
8 cloves garlic, crushed
1 sprig of thyme
1 sprig of marjoram
salt
1 bay leaf
2 chillies

Pour hot water over the meat, drain, dry on paper towel and cut into cubes. Mix together the ingredients for the marinade. Place the meat in the marinade, preferably in an earthenware dish, and refrigerate for 2 – 3 days. Drain, and reserve the marinade.

Melt the oil and the lard in a heavy saucepan and add the meat and two-thirds of the marinade. Simmer until the meat is cooked. Turn up the heat and fry the meat, then add the rest of the marinade.

Place slices of bread over the meat, cover and simmer until the sauce has thickened.

Garnish with orange slices and serve with fried new potatoes and roast sweet potatoes.

**Serves 4 – 6.**


**Variation**
The bread may be dipped in the marinade and fried, and the potatoes may be cooked with the meat rather than fried separately.

# Pork Belly *Vovô*-style
## *Barriga de Porco à Moda do Vovô*

Another of my father's specialities.

1 kg pork belly
20 ml coarse salt

*Sauce*
5 – 6 cloves garlic, chopped
125 ml chopped parsley

50 ml chopped coriander
100 ml olive oil
25 ml vinegar
15 ml lemon juice
piri piri to taste

Cut slits in the meat and rind (crackling). Sprinkle with coarse salt and leave for 30 minutes. Braai over coals until tender and very crisp. Scrape the charred rind, cut the meat into small pieces and place in a bowl.

Mix together the ingredients for the sauce and pour over the meat. Leave for 15 minutes before serving.

**Serves 4.**

# Roast Fillet of Pork
## *Lombo de Porco Assado*

There are many variations of this tasty dish. The easiest is to rub the fillet with a paste of garlic, salt, pepper or piri piri, a bay leaf and a little oil. Leave for a few hours, then pour 250 ml white wine over the pork and roast at 220° C for 30 – 35 minutes.

The most unusual version is the recipe that follows.

1 pork fillet (about 800 g)
500 g clams
100 g fresh breadcrumbs
200 ml liquid (half milk and
    half liquid from clams)
25 ml butter
1 spring onion, chopped
3 egg yolks
2 ml ground nutmeg
10 ml lemon juice
salt and pepper
125 ml wine

*Garlic paste*
2 cloves garlic, crushed
salt and pepper to taste
10 ml olive oil
10 ml wine
5 ml thyme
piri piri to taste

Cut the fillet open lengthwise and flatten slightly with a meat mallet. Mix together the ingredients for the garlic paste and rub it over the meat.

Soak the clams (as described on p55), open them, remove the shells, strain and reserve the liquid. Soak the breadcrumbs in 100 ml milk mixed with 100 ml liquid from the clams.

In a saucepan melt the butter and sauté the chopped spring onion. Remove from the heat. Add the egg yolks, nutmeg, lemon juice and clams. Check the seasoning. If necessary, add a little salt and pepper. Place this mixture in the centre of the fillet, fold over and tie with string. Place in a roasting pan, add any left-over garlic paste and pour the wine over the meat. Roast at 180° C for 45 – 60 minutes.

Pork fillet is usually served with fried potatoes and *esparregado* (see p 103).
**Serves 4.**

# Roast Leg of Pork
## *Perna de Porco Assada*

1 leg pork (2 kg)
5 – 6 cloves garlic, whole
fresh thyme

*Paste*
50 ml lard
25 ml oil
10 ml paprika
20 ml red pepper paste (see p194)
salt and pepper
2 cloves garlic, crushed
100 ml white wine

Make incisions in the meat with a sharp knife. Place a clove of garlic and a sprig of thyme into each slit. Mix together the ingredients for the paste. Score the rind and rub the paste over the meat. Leave overnight. Place the meat fat side up on a rack inside the roasting pan. Roast at 160° C for 2 – 3 hours. Baste occasionally with the sauce in the roasting pan. Turn the meat and place under a grill for 5 – 10 minutes before serving.
**Serves 6 – 8.**

# Suckling Pig
## *Leitão*

Note that the preparation of this dish starts three days in advance . . . and make sure that your oven is large enough to accommodate the piglet. The piglet may be stuffed and stitched before roasting.

| | |
|---|---|
| 1 suckling pig (6 – 8 kg) | ***Paste*** |
| cold water | 60 ml coarse salt |
| 20 ml salt | 30 cloves garlic, pressed |
| lemon and orange slices | 50 – 100 piri piri chillies (this is *not* a printing error!) |
| | 25 ml olive oil |
| | 125 ml wine |
| | 100 g lard |
| | 100 g butter |

Wipe the suckling pig thoroughly, remove any hair and clean around the mouth and eyes. Leave to soak overnight in cold water, salt, orange and lemon slices.

Next day dry the meat thoroughly, both inside and out, with a clean dish cloth. Make the paste (easily done by blending all the ingredients in a food processor) and rub this over the piglet – again, both inside and out. Leave overnight.

Make a trellis of bay sticks or use a rack inside the roasting pan to prevent the rind from becoming soggy. Place the piglet on the trellis, covering the ears, tail and feet with tin foil. Roast for 4 – 5 hours at 160° C.

**Serves 20 people.**

# Lamb, Mutton, Kid and Goat
## *Anho, Carneiro, Cabrito e Cabra*

Each region in Portugal has its preference for one or other of the above kinds of meat. Most of the recipes can be made using any one of them.

# Lamb Stew
# *Carneiro Guisado*

2 kg stewing lamb
25 ml olive oil
10 ml cooking oil
2 onions, chopped
3 tomatoes, grated
2 green peppers, diced
3 cloves garlic, crushed
2 bay leaves
5 ml paprika

2 cloves
1 sprig of parsley
salt and pepper
500 g potatoes
500 g green beans, sliced
5 ml vinegar
500 g day-old bread
mint leaves

Cut the meat into cubes. Heat the oils in a deep casserole. Brown the meat and then add the onions, tomatoes, green peppers, garlic, bay leaves, paprika, cloves, parsley and seasoning. Simmer for 20 – 25 minutes, adding a little water when necessary.

Peel and cut the potatoes and add to the stew. Add the sliced green beans, cover and cook until tender. Add the vinegar just before serving.

Cut the bread into thin slices and place in a soup tureen with the mint leaves. Pour the broth over the bread and serve the meat and vegetables in a separate dish.

**Serves 6 – 8.**

# Roast Lamb or Kid with Rice
## *Cabrito no Forno*

The meat must be extremely tender. Because clay ovens are still in use in Portugal a whole lamb (4 – 5 kg) is often cooked. A special clay dish is used to cook the rice. We have to be more practical to suit our home ovens, hence my adaptation of this recipe. If you are using kid, remember to soak it overnight in cold water to which salt, lemon slices, peppercorns and bay leaves have been added.

1,5 kg boned shoulder or leg
   of lamb or kid
1 litre stock
500 ml rice
3 ml turmeric
bay sticks
60 ml Port wine ⎫
100 ml white wine ⎭ for basting

*Paste*
5 ml paprika
3 cloves garlic, chopped
1 bay leaf
1 small bunch chopped parsley
10 ml coarse salt

pepper
15 ml olive oil
10 ml lard
1 onion, chopped

*Stock*
250 g lamb knuckle (or use the
   bones from the leg or
   shoulder)
100 g spek or bacon
100 g *presunto*
3 – 4 slices *chouriço*
1 sprig of parsley
2 cloves
5 peppercorns

Mix together the ingredients for the paste. Rub the paste well into the meat and leave for 4 – 6 hours.

Place the ingredients for the stock in a large saucepan and simmer until the meats are cooked. Strain and reserve both stock and meats.

Measure out 1 litre of stock (enough to cook 500 ml rice). Place the rice in an ovenproof tray, add the hot stock and turmeric and stir well. Make a trivet with bay sticks (use wooden spoons if nothing else is available) and place it over the tray containing the rice. Place the meat on the trivet and roast in an oven preheated to 160° C for 1 – 1 ½ hours. Baste and turn the meat frequently, using a mixture of the Port and white wines and any left-over paste for basting. Add more stock to the rice if necessary. Add the cut-up meats from the stock to the rice just before serving.

**Serves 6 – 8.**

# Roast Leg of Lamb
## *Perna de Carneiro Assada no Forno*

1 leg of lamb (2 kg)
salt and pepper
10 ml paprika
50 g butter *or* margarine
25 ml olive oil
2 onions, sliced

2 cloves garlic, crushed
1 tomato, sliced
1 bay leaf
200 ml white wine
500 g new potatoes

Rub the lamb with salt, pepper and paprika. Melt the butter and oil in a roasting pan. Place the meat in the hot fat and brown on both sides. Cover the meat with the onions, garlic, tomato, bay leaf and wine and place in an oven preheated to 160° C.

Half-way through the cooking time (ie after about an hour) add the new potatoes and baste frequently with the sauce in the roasting pan.

**Serves 6 – 8.**

# Lamb Chops
## *Costeletas de Carneiro*

2 onions, chopped
2 cloves garlic, crushed
25 ml olive oil
25 ml chopped parsley
25 ml paprika

1 kg lamb or mutton chops
100 ml fresh breadcrumbs
salt to taste
500 g potatoes, cubed
10 ml vinegar

Fry the onions and garlic in the oil until soft. Add the parsley and paprika and stir well. Add the chops and fry for a few minutes. Add the breadcrumbs and salt and enough water to cover the chops. Simmer for 20 – 25 minutes. Add the potatoes and continue cooking until the meat and potatoes are tender. If necessary, mash a few potatoes to thicken the gravy. Add the vinegar just before serving.

**Serves 4 – 6.**

# Goat Stew Angola-style
## *Caldeirada de Cabrito à Angolana*

This was a popular dish in the Angolan interior and sometimes game was used instead of goat. This is usually a very 'hot' dish, so do not be shy with the chillies.

| | |
|---|---|
| 1,5 kg goat | 1 kg potatoes, sliced |
| 5 cloves garlic, pressed | 20 ml oil |
| *gindungo* (piri piri) to taste | 500 ml sparkling wine |
| salt | (champagne – why not?) |
| 6 onions, sliced | 2 green peppers, cut into strips |
| 6 tomatoes, sliced | 1 sprig of parsley |

Cut the meat into serving pieces. Pour boiling water over the meat and then rinse in cold water. Rub the meat with the garlic, piri piri and salt.

Place a layer of onion at the bottom of a large casserole, followed by layers of tomatoes, meat and potatoes. Repeat the layers, ending with a layer of onion and tomato. Pour the oil and the sparkling wine into the casserole. Place strips of green pepper and parsley on top, cover and simmer until cooked (1 – 1 ½ hours). This dish may also be baked in an oven preheated to 170° C for about 2 hours, but do not stir it. If necessary, shake the pot slightly.

**Serves 6 – 8.**

# Oven Stew
## *Chanfana ou Lampantana*

This dish was typical of the Beira provinces in Mozambique where it was served at large gatherings such as weddings and christenings. For the best results one should use a black earthenware casserole made from *Molelos* clay and a clay oven. I use a black iron pot and a very hot electric oven . . . and I still feed the crowds. This dish is best prepared a day in advance and reheated. Lamb may be used instead of goat.

| | |
|---|---|
| 2,5 – 3 kg goat, cut into large | 2 ml ground nutmeg |
| pieces | 1 bay leaf |
| 120 g bacon, diced | 1 sprig of parsley |
| 125 ml olive oil | 3 cloves garlic, crushed |
| 25 ml lard | salt and pepper |

| | |
|---|---|
| 2 onions, sliced | piri piri (optional) |
| 5 ml paprika | 3 – 4 litres *Bairrada* or any red |
| 2 ml ground cloves | wine |

Place the meat and bacon in a pot and add the oil and lard. Add the onions, spices, herbs and seasonings. Cover completely with the wine.

Cover the pot and place it in a very hot oven (200° C) for 1 hour. Remove the lid and stir. Add more wine if necessary. Cover the pot again and reduce the oven temperature to 100° C. Continue cooking, preferably overnight or until the meat is tender. (The time taken will depend on the age of the lamb or goat.) Serve with potatoes boiled in their jackets.

**Serves 6 – 8.**

## Other Meat Dishes

# Boiled Meat and Vegetables
## *Cozido à Mimi*

This recipe differs from region to region, depending on the availability of ingredients. I have used just about all the ingredients possible, resulting in a hearty dish for cold winter days.

| | |
|---|---|
| 1 pork sausage | 1 clove garlic |
| 1 blood sausage | salt and pepper |
| 1 pork trotter | 1 small cabbage, cut in half |
| 500 g lamb knuckles | 4 – 6 potatoes, halved |
| 500 g short ribs or shin | 1 sweet potato, quartered |
| half a chicken (optional) | 500 g green beans |
| 500 g chick peas, soaked | 500 g pumpkin, cut into |
| overnight and drained | 4 – 6 pieces |
| 125 ml olive oil | 125 ml small pasta shapes |
| 1 tomato | 250 ml rice |
| 1 onion | mint leaves |

Place all the meats, the chick peas, oil, tomato, onion, garlic and seasoning in a large pot. Cover with cold water and bring to the boil. Simmer until almost cooked – about 1 hour. Add the cabbage. Continue simmering for 30 minutes and then add the remaining vegetables. Cook until all the vegetables are tender.

Drain the liquid and divide it for soup and for cooking the rice. *Soup:* Add more water if necessary, bring to the boil and add the small pasta shapes. Continue simmering until the pasta is cooked. *Rice:* Cook in 500 ml of the drained broth.

*To serve:* First serve the soup, adding mint leaves. Place the rice in the centre of a large serving platter. Arrange the cut up meats on one side of the dish and the vegetables on the other.

**Serves 8 – 10.**

# Liver Slices
## *Iscas com Elas*

This used to be a very popular dish in the Lisbon district but its popularity seems to have diminished in the modern diet. *Elas* refers to the potatoes which are a must when serving this dish.

| | |
|---|---|
| 500 g calf's liver (pork liver can also be used) | 3 onions, sliced |
| oil and butter for frying | 10 ml paprika |
| 500 g boiled potatoes | 5 ml salt |
| | pepper or piri piri to taste |
| | 10 ml olive oil |
| *Marinade* | 5 – 6 cloves garlic, crushed |
| 100 ml white wine | pinch of ground nutmeg |
| 50 ml red wine | 1 sprig of parsley |
| 20 ml vinegar | |

Remove the skin from the liver and cut it into slices. Mix together the ingredients for the marinade, pour over the liver and leave for a couple of hours or even overnight (depends on how hungry you are).

Remove the liver from the marinade and fry it in a mixture of oil and butter. Remove from the pan and keep warm. Drain the onions from the marinade and fry them separately.

Arrange thick slices of boiled potatoes on a large platter, place the liver on top of the potatoes, and top with the fried onions. Add the marinade to the frying pan, bring to the boil and pour over the liver.

**Serves 4.**

# Braised Tongue
## *Lingua Estufada à Portuguesa*

Legend says that if you eat the tip of the tongue you will be a good speaker. Perhaps this is why the Portuguese talk so fast and so much!

| | |
|---|---|
| 1 ox tongue (900 g – 1 kg) | 20 ml butter |
| 1 onion | 10 small onions |
| 1 carrot | 250 ml red or white wine |
| 3 cloves | 25 ml Madeira wine |
| 1 bay leaf | 3 tomatoes, grated |
| 1 sprig of parsley | 10 ml paprika |
| salt | salt and pepper |
| 100 g bacon, diced | |

Soak the tongue in cold water for 2 hours. Drain. Pour boiling water over the tongue and remove skin. Wash well. Place the tongue in a pot with the onion, carrot, cloves, bay leaf, parsley and salt. Cover with water and cook until tender – about 1 – 1 1/2 hours. Remove the tongue and drain.

In a second pot fry the bacon in the butter, add the small onions and the whole tongue. Add the wines, tomatoes and paprika and simmer until the sauce is rich and thick. Taste, and adjust seasoning. Remove the tongue and slice it. Place the tongue slices on a platter and pour the sauce over them. Serve with the small onions, cubes of fried potato, and green peas.

**Serves 4 – 6.**

# Tripe Porto-style
## *Tripas à Moda do Porto*

Although it is not the most glamorous of nicknames, the inhabitants of Porto are very proud of being called *tripeiros* (tripe-eaters). The name derives from an act of extreme patriotism and generosity.

During the fifteenth century Henry the Navigator provisioned the ships that conquered North Africa with all the available meat in Porto, leaving only the tripe for the local inhabitants. The people made the best of it, turning it into a 'banquet dish'. A similar dish, called *dobrada,* is made in other parts of Portugal.

There are probably as many recipes for tripe as there are inhabitants of Porto – and it is a very large city. The use of a pressure cooker really helps with the recipe given below. If you do not have one I suggest you start cooking two days in advance. The help of your local butcher might be needed to cut and saw the bones. I have modified the recipe somewhat because some of the traditional ingredients are not available locally. The end result is worth the time and effort involved. Veal tripe is best, but it is not always available. Nowadays one can obtain ready-to-cook tripe but I still prefer to soak it in water and lemon slices for a couple of hours. (My husband says that I soak it and rinse it so many times that it has no flavour left.)

| | |
|---|---|
| 800 g tripe | 2 carrots, diced |
| 1 orange, sliced | 2 bay leaves |
| 1 lemon, sliced | 20 ml chopped parsley |
| 500 g butter beans, soaked overnight | 10 ml paprika |
| | 2 ml ground cumin |
| 1 pork knuckle, salted overnight | 2 ml ground cloves |
| | 2 ml turmeric |
| 1 veal trotter | 500 ml tomatoes, grated |
| 35 ml olive oil | 100 ml white wine |
| 100 g *chouriço*, sliced | salt and pepper |
| 100 g *presunto,* cubed | piri piri to taste |
| 4 onions, chopped | half a chicken, cut into small |
| 3 cloves garlic, crushed | pieces |

Soak the tripe in cold water with orange and lemon slices for a couple of hours. Rinse and cook in salted water for 3 – 4 hours or until tender.

Drain the beans, cover with fresh water and cook until almost tender. Drain, and reserve the liquid. Rinse the trotter and knuckle, cover with water and boil until tender. In a large pot heat the oil and add the *chouriço, presunto,* onions, garlic, carrots, bay leaves, parsley and spices. Simmer for 5 – 8 minutes. Add the tomatoes and wine and season with salt, pepper and piri piri. Simmer until a thick gravy is obtained. Add a little bean or meat stock if necessary.

Cut up the tripe, trotter, knuckle and chicken and place in the gravy. Add a little bean or meat stock if necessary. Simmer for 20 minutes. Add the beans and simmer for a further 15 minutes. Be careful not to overcook.

Serve with white rice and *broa* (see p152). (Did I forget the wine?)

**Serves 6 – 8.**

# Poultry and Game
## *Aves e Caça*

Portuguese men are very fond of game-shooting. In Portugal the hunting season lasts from October to December and, believe me, there are more hunters than birds. One year I was driving up to Lisbon on the day the hunting season opened and I could not believe the exodus from the city in the direction of the Alentejo and the Algarve . . . work does not seem to matter while there are birds to be hunted. Partridges and *tordos* are very popular, as are wild rabbits.

In South Africa, Portuguese men hunt guinea fowl, wild duck and sometimes large game. The saying goes, 'If you can't beat them join them', and this is exactly what I did. Fed up with staying at home every weekend during the hunting season, I joined the hunters – first for the exercise and fresh air, then as an observer, and later I was promoted to 'one of the boys'. Now I have a double job on my hands . . . hunting *and* preparing the fare.

# Hunter's Rabbit
## *Coelho à Caçador*

Rabbits are farm-raised and popular in Portugal – the flavour is very similar to chicken. This recipe may be used for wild rabbit, when available. Wild rabbit should be soaked in salted water for a couple of hours after cleaning. Keep the liver and add it to the sauce just before adding the olives.

| | |
|---|---|
| 1 small rabbit | *Marinade* |
| 2 onions, chopped | 3 cloves garlic, crushed |
| 50 ml bacon, diced | 1 bay leaf |
| 50 ml olive oil | 5 ml salt |
| 20 ml butter *or* margarine | pepper |
| 2 tomatoes, grated | 250 ml white wine |
| rabbit liver, if available | 250 ml red wine |
| 60 ml strong black coffee | sprinkling of fresh herbs |
| 1 tot whisky | 5 ml paprika |
| 8 – 10 olives, pitted | |
| fried bread | |
| chopped parsley | |

Mix together the ingredients for the marinade. Cut the rabbit into serving pieces. Place it in the marinade overnight. Drain, and reserve the marinade. Fry the onions and chopped bacon in the olive oil and butter. Add the rabbit pieces and fry until brown. Add the tomatoes and the marinade and simmer for about 30 minutes. Add the very finely chopped liver and the coffee and whisky. Cook for a further 5 minutes. Add the olives just before serving.

Garnish with triangles of fried bread (cut each slice into 4) dipped in parsley. Serve with small fried or boiled potatoes.

**Serves 4.**

# Braised Guinea Fowl
## *Galinhola no Tacho*

1 – 2 guinea fowl, cut into pieces
100 g *presunto*, diced
10 ml garlic butter (see p124)
10 ml lard (optional)
25 ml olive oil
1 onion, chopped
25 ml Madeira wine
fresh thyme, chopped

*Marinade*
1 tot whisky
1 tot brandy

500 ml red wine
50 ml vinegar
4 – 5 cloves garlic, crushed
8 peppercorns
4 cloves
4 allspice
1 bay leaf
4 – 5 piri piri
1 ml ground nutmeg
10 ml paprika
2 ml ground cumin
10 ml olive oil

Mix together the ingredients for the marinade. Place the guinea fowl pieces in the marinade and leave for 24 hours. Remove the guinea fowl from the marinade, drain and reserve the liquid. Using a deep frying pan with a lid, fry the diced *presunto* in the garlic butter, lard and olive oil. Add the guinea fowl pieces and brown. (This may be done in batches.) Add the onion and some of the marinade. Simmer very gently, adding more marinade as necessary, until the guinea fowl is cooked – at least 1 hour. If necessary, add a little more red wine.

Just before serving, add the Madeira wine and the fresh thyme. Serve with cubes of fried potato.

**Serves 4 – 6.**

# Guinea Fowl Breast Fillets
## *Peito de Galinhola*

These are even more delicious than chicken breasts. With a little practice, patience and a good knife the flesh is very easily removed from the bone. (Easy for me to say when I have a husband who does it so expertly!) Once the flesh has been removed from the bone, slice it into steaks approximately 1 centimetre thick. One guinea fowl yields about six steaks.

6 guinea fowl steaks
oil and butter for frying

*Marinade*
3 cloves garlic, chopped
a few sprigs of thyme
5 ml paprika

1 ml ground cumin
salt and piri piri to taste
1 bay leaf
20 ml olive oil
125 ml white wine
1 tot whisky

Mix together the ingredients for the marinade. Pour over the guinea fowl steaks and leave for 24 hours. (They can be frozen in the marinade for up to 2 months.) Fry the drained steaks in a mixture of oil and butter.
**Serves 4 – 6.**

# Piri Piri Chicken
## *Galinha à Piri Piri*

Take a nostalgic trip to the LM of a bygone era . . . invite your friends and enjoy Chicken Piri Piri out of doors with lots of *vinho verde*.

2 medium-sized chickens
    (1 – 1,2 kg each)
salt and pepper
100 g soft margarine *or* butter
whole piri piri, crushed (3 – 5
    for medium strength, 5 – 10
    for hot)

10 ml lemon juice
2 – 4 cloves garlic, crushed
5 ml paprika *(colorau)*
12,5 ml olive oil

Clean the chickens and spatchcock (cut open through the back and flatten). Slit through the thick parts of the chicken. Make a paste out of all the other ingredients and rub it over the inside and outside of the chicken. Rest the chicken for 2 hours. Grill or braai, basting the chicken with the paste every time it is turned.

**Serves 4 – 6.**

Serve with the following sauce:

| | |
|---|---|
| 20 ml butter (plus 12,5 ml olive oil – optional) | piri piri to taste |
| 2 cloves garlic | juice of half a lemon |
| | 5 ml chopped parsley |

Fry the garlic in the butter. Add the piri piri, lemon juice and parsley. Remove the garlic and serve.

# Chicken Mozambique
## *Galinha Mozambique*

Another version of Chicken Piri Piri.

| | |
|---|---|
| 6 cloves garlic, pressed | 500 ml coconut milk (see p125) |
| 10 ml salt | 2 medium-sized chickens |
| 2 bay leaves | juice of 1 lemon |
| 5 ml paprika | 125 g butter |
| piri piri to taste | 50 ml olive oil |

In a large bowl, mix the garlic, salt, bay leaves, paprika and piri piri to a paste. Add the coconut milk. Cut the chickens in half and slit through the thighs, drumsticks and breasts. Place the chicken in the coconut milk marinade for at least 6 – 8 hours, turning often.

Remove the chicken from the marinade. Mix the marinade with the lemon juice, butter and oil. Bring to the boil and use this mixture to baste the chicken which should be grilled over medium coals. Serve the chicken with any remaining marinade.

**Serves 4.**

(Try this recipe with prawns instead of chicken, but don't invite anyone to share them with you . . . )

# Chicken Curry
## *Chacuti de Galinha*

This is a traditional recipe from the former Portuguese colony of Goa.

100 ml desiccated coconut
10 ml coriander seeds
5 ml cumin seeds
10 peppercorns
1 bay leaf
5 cloves
5 ml turmeric
10 ml chopped ginger
1 stick cinnamon
4 dried red chillies
5 ml nutmeg

5 ml mustard seeds
4 cardamom seeds
5 ml fennel seeds
6 cloves garlic, crushed
2 kg chicken
3 onions, chopped
25 ml cooking oil
2 chicken stock cubes
500 ml coconut milk (see p125)
coconut chunks (optional)

Place the desiccated coconut in a frying pan and stir continuously over medium heat until golden. Transfer to kitchen paper. Place all the spices, the bay leaf and the garlic in the same frying pan and roast lightly. Transfer the coconut and the spices to a food processor and blend until a paste is formed.

Cut the chicken into serving pieces. Fry the onions in the oil. Add the chicken and fry until golden. Add the spice mixture, the stock cubes, the coconut milk and the coconut chunks. Simmer until the chicken is cooked. Serve with white rice.

**Serves 6 – 8.**

# Jugged Chicken
## *Frango na Púcara*

This is a very popular recipe from the Alcobaça region, famous for its pottery – hence the decorative terracotta 'jugs' used for making this dish.

1 medium-sized chicken (about
   1 kg)
25 ml olive oil
10 ml paprika
salt and pepper to taste
10 small onions
200 g *presunto*, diced
2 tomatoes, chopped

4 cloves garlic, crushed
1 sprig of parsley
2 bay leaves
250 ml white wine
60 ml Port wine
25 ml *aguardente*
  half a chicken stock cube

Clean the chicken, including the body cavity, and leave whole. Rub the chicken with a mixture of the oil, paprika, salt and pepper. Place any left-over mixture and a few onions in the body cavity. Place half the *presunto* in the 'jug' or an ovenproof casserole. Place the whole chicken on top and surround it with the onions, tomatoes and the rest of the *presunto*. Mix the remaining ingredients together and pour over the chicken.

    Cover the dish and bake in an oven preheated to 180° C for 30 – 45 minutes. Remove the lid and bake for a further 15 minutes. If there is still a large amount of liquid in the dish pour it into a saucepan, bring to the boil and reduce until it is thick. Serve with thinly sliced potato chips.

    **Serves 4 – 6.**

# Jugged Chicken with Cabbage
## *Frango na Púcara com Couves*

The proper container for cooking this dish is a deep terracotta jug. If this is not available use a deep casserole dish.

1 medium-sized chicken
salt and pepper to taste
10 ml paprika
3 – 4 cloves garlic, pressed
125 ml white wine
25 ml olive oil
25 ml lard (optional)
25 g *presunto*, finely diced

1 onion, chopped
1 bay leaf
45 ml tomato purée
1 chicken stock cube, dissolved
   in 100 ml water
1 sugarloaf cabbage
500 g new potatoes (optional)

Clean the chicken and cut it into 8 pieces. Season with salt, pepper, paprika and garlic. Pour over the wine and marinate for 10 minutes. Drain the chicken and reserve the marinade. Place the oil, lard and *presunto* in a frying pan and brown the chicken on both sides. Remove the chicken. Add to the pan the onion, bay leaf, tomato purée, chicken stock and the marinade. Simmer for 2 – 3 minutes.

Place the chicken, the quartered cabbage and the potatoes in a deep casserole dish. Pour over the sauce. Cover and simmer for 30 – 40 minutes.

**Serves 4 – 6.**

# Brown Chicken Stew
## *Galinha de Cabidela*

Let me warn you that this recipe is not for the faint-hearted. Everyone to whom I have served this dish has enjoyed it until I have told them what is in it . . . Although chicken is most commonly used in the recipe, turkey or rabbit can be substituted. In some regions potatoes are used instead of rice.

| | |
|---|---|
| 1 home-slaughtered chicken | 1 stick cinnamon |
| 20 ml vinegar | 1 clove |
| 20 ml white wine | 1 bay leaf |
| 50 ml olive oil | 1 chicken stock cube, dissolved |
| 2 onions, chopped |   in 500 ml water |
| 2 cloves garlic, crushed | parsley, pepper and salt |
| 1 tomato, grated | 500 ml rice *or* 4 – 6 potatoes |
| 5 ml paprika | |

Place the chicken blood in a cup and mix it with the vinegar and wine to prevent it from coagulating. Cut the chicken into pieces.

In a large pot, fry the onions and garlic in the olive oil. Add the tomato, the spices, bay leaf, chicken stock, seasonings, and the chicken pieces. Simmer until the chicken is half-cooked. Add the rice or potatoes and sufficient water to cook them. When the rice or potatoes are cooked, add a little of the hot liquid from the pot to the vinegar and blood mixture and then stir it into the pot. Simmer for 2 – 3 minutes and then serve.

**Serves 6 – 8.**

# Chicken Muamba
## *Muamba de Galinha*

A traditional Angolan dish, *Muambada* is the name given to the meal when *Muamba* is served. Although chicken is usually used, fish is an acceptable substitute. Palm oil and okra give this dish its very distinctive taste. The traditional recipe calls for *abobóra-carneira*, which is a type of pumpkin that is not available locally. I use courgettes or brinjals instead.

20 ml olive oil
50 ml palm oil
1 large chicken, cut into portions
3 onions, chopped
2 cloves garlic, chopped
3 tomatoes, grated
1 bay leaf
15 ml lemon juice

piri piri *(gindungo)* to taste
250 g courgettes or brinjals
15 – 20 okra (use tinned ones if
    not available fresh)

*Serve with Funge*
250 g mealie meal
salt
1 litre water

Place the oils and the chicken in a large pan. Add the rest of the ingredients, except the vegetables. Mix well and simmer over a low heat until the chicken is nearly cooked. Add the courgettes or brinjals and, lastly, the okra. Just before serving check the seasoning, and if necessary thicken the gravy with a little mealie meal. Serve with mealie meal cooked to a soft consistency (see p116).

**Serves 4.**

# Mimi's Chicken
## *Galinha à Mimi*

Anyone who has been to my classes has used this recipe again and again. Although it is not from the 'traditional' range, it is one that can be made to feed a large crowd, especially when a meal-in-one is required.

1 large chicken (with giblets),
    cut into portions
25 ml olive oil
2 onions, chopped
2 tomatoes, grated

10 ml paprika
500 ml rice
1 chicken stock cube
1,5 ml boiling water
250 g frozen peas ✓

1 bay leaf

1 red pepper, cubed

1 green pepper, cubed

1 carrot, diced

2 sticks celery, chopped

1 ml turmeric

chopped parsley or coriander
leaves

*Marinade*

3 cloves garlic, crushed

salt, pepper and piri piri to taste

10 ml lemon juice

Mix together the ingredients for the marinade and marinate the chicken pieces for 1 hour. Fry the onions in the olive oil, add the tomatoes, bay leaf, peppers, carrot, celery, turmeric, paprika and chicken giblets. Cook for 1 – 2 minutes. Add the rice and stir well. Dissolve the chicken cube in the boiling water and add to the pan. Add the peas and stir well.

Pour into a deep ovenproof dish. Arrange the chicken pieces, skin side down, on top of the rice. Bake at 180° C for 1 hour. Turn the chicken pieces and add more water if necessary. Bake for a further 30 minutes to brown the chicken. Just before serving sprinkle with chopped parsley or coriander leaves.

**Serves 6 – 8.**

**The next two recipes are useful for using up chicken left over from soup-making.**

# Fried Chicken
## *Galinha Cerejada*

25 ml olive oil

20 g butter (or garlic butter
if available)

1 cooked chicken, cut into
pieces

6 – 8 cloves garlic

60 ml white wine

Heat the oil and butter in a frying pan. Add the chicken pieces and fry until brown and crusty on both sides. Add the whole unpeeled, lightly crushed (use your fist!) garlic and the white wine. Simmer for 2 minutes and serve.

**Serves 4 – 6.**

**Variation**

Try adding a few banana halves to the pan just before adding the garlic.

# Chicken Fricassee
## *Galinha de Fricassé*

Surprise, no olive oil! It would spoil the delicate taste.

25 ml butter
2 onions, chopped
1 cooked chicken, cut into
   pieces (bones may be removed)
2 egg yolks

5 ml lemon juice
250 ml chicken stock
salt and pepper
chopped parsley

Melt the butter in a frying pan, add the onion and sauté until soft but not brown. Add the chicken pieces and cook for 2 – 3 minutes. Beat the egg yolks with the lemon juice and stock. Add to the chicken, season, and then simmer over a very low heat for just long enough to cook the egg yolks without curdling them. Sprinkle with chopped parsley and serve at once with plain white rice or mashed potatoes.

**Serves 4 – 6.**

# Chicken Roulade
## *Torta de Galinha*

1 kg potatoes
50 g butter
15 ml cornflour (maizena)
salt and pepper
200 ml warm milk
5 eggs, separated

*Filling*
500 ml cooked chicken, diced
1 tin onion and tomato mix
salt and pepper
5 ml dried herbs (oregano,
   thyme)
125 ml chicken stock (half a
   stock cube + 125 ml boiling
   water)

Cook and mash the potatoes. Add the butter, maizena, salt, pepper and warm milk and beat well. Add the beaten egg yolks and then fold in the stiffly beaten egg whites. Spread the mixture in a lined Swiss-roll pan and bake at 200° C for 20 – 25 minutes. Do not overbake as this will make it very difficult to roll.

Meanwhile, prepare the filling. Combine all the ingredients for the filling in a saucepan and simmer over a low heat for 10 – 15 minutes. Adjust the seasoning.

Place a wet kitchen cloth on a board and cover it with wax paper. Sprinkle the paper with breadcrumbs. Very carefully, turn the baked roulade out of the pan and on to the breadcrumbs. Cut away the crusts from the sides and ends of the roulade. Spread the filling over the roulade and roll as you would a Swiss roll. Pour any left-over filling over the roll. Serve hot or cold as a snack, or as a light meal with a salad.

**Serves 4.**

# Chicken with Pumpkin Seeds
## *Xin-xin ou Chim-chin*

Our chicken is travelling once more – this time to Brazil. This is an Afro-Brazilian recipe that dates from the time of the slave trade.

1,5 kg chicken
salt to taste
750 ml water
60 ml palm oil (olive oil
   may be substituted)
100 ml prawns, cooked and minced
125 ml chopped parsley
2 onions, chopped
2 – 3 chillies, chopped
2 ml Tabasco sauce
100 g pumpkin seeds, shelled,
   roasted and ground

10 ml ground coriander
50 ml cooking oil
fresh coriander leaves
whole pumpkin seeds, roasted

*Serve with rice cooked in*
*coconut milk*
500 ml rice
750 ml water
250 ml coconut milk (see p125)
salt to taste

Cut the chicken into serving pieces and stew in a covered saucepan with the salt, water, palm oil, prawns, parsley, onions, chillies and Tabasco sauce for about 30 minutes. Remove the lid, reduce the heat and continue simmering until most of the liquid has evaporated. Add the ground pumpkin seeds, ground coriander and oil. Fry the chicken until golden.

Arrange the cooked rice in the shape of a pyramid in a deep serving dish. (The idea is that it should resemble the Sugarloaf Mountain – *Pão de Açúcar*.) Pour the chicken very carefully over the rice. Garnish with chopped coriander leaves and whole roasted pumpkin seeds.

**Serves 6 – 8.**

# Chicken stuffed with Chestnut Purée
## *Frango Recheado com Castanhas*

1 large (about 2 kg) chicken, deboned

**Stuffing**
250 g chestnut purée
250 g pork loin, minced
250 g veal, minced
2 eggs
10 olives, pitted
3 spring onions, chopped

175 ml fresh breadcrumbs
2 cloves garlic, crushed
salt and pepper
a few sprigs of fresh herbs

**Basting sauce**
50 ml butter
10 ml paprika
25 ml white wine

Make the stuffing first. Slit the chestnuts, place in salted water and cook until tender. Remove the outer and inner skins and purée in a blender. Add the rest of the ingredients for the stuffing to the chestnut purée and stir well.

Stuff the chicken and sew it together with string. Make the basting sauce by melting the butter in a saucepan and then adding the paprika and wine.

Place the stuffed chicken in a cooking bag and pour in the basting sauce. Tie off the cooking bag and make a few holes in it. Roast the chicken at 180° C for about 1 1/2 hours. Serve hot or cold – it is easier to cut when cold.
**Serves 6 – 8.**

# Duck with Rice
## *Arroz de Pato*

2 litres cold water
1 medium-sized duck with
   giblets
1 *chouriço* (about 70 g), sliced
250 g *presunto,* sliced
8 peppercorns
1 small carrot

1 bay leaf
2 cloves garlic
1 onion
500 ml rice
1 egg yolk, beaten with a little
   water
melted butter

Place the cold water, duck giblets, wings and neck, *chouriço, presunto,* peppercorns, carrot, bay leaf, garlic and onion in a large saucepan. Simmer for 1 hour. Strain and reserve both the liquid and the meats. Place the duck in the strained stock and simmer until almost cooked (45 minutes – 1 hour). Remove the duck and strain the stock through muslin (if available) – this will remove most of the fat.

Cook the rice in 1 litre of the duck stock. Cut the duck into serving portions, removing most of the bones. Place the duck in an ovenproof tray.

Pour 250 ml of the stock over the duck and place in an oven preheated to 200° C for 15 – 20 minutes.

Meanwhile, remove any meat from the wings and neck, chop the giblets and add to the rice. When the rice is cooked, spoon it over the duck in the baking tray, covering the duck completely. Brush with the egg yolk mixture and arrange the *chouriço* and *presunto* slices neatly on top of the rice. Drizzle melted butter over the rice. Bake for 15 – 20 minutes at 200° C until golden.

**Serves 6 – 8.**

# Stuffed Turkey
## *Peru Recheado*

1 frozen turkey
25 ml coarse salt
lemon and orange slices
30 g lard
1 Portuguese sausage, minced
salt and pepper
10 ml paprika
bacon strips
125 ml Port wine

*First stuffing*
25 ml butter
750 g sweet potato, cooked and
    mashed
1 egg
10 olives, pitted
salt and pepper
10 g pine kernels

*Second stuffing*
30 g butter
1 onion, chopped
turkey giblets, minced
2 pork or beef sausages, skinned
50 g breadcrumbs
salt, pepper and nutmeg

Clean the turkey and place in water with the coarse salt and lemon and orange slices for 2 – 3 hours. (Place in the refrigerator in hot weather.) Drain and dry the inside and outside of the turkey with a kitchen cloth. Fill the neck cavity with the first stuffing and the body cavity with the second stuffing.

*To make the first stuffing:* Melt the butter in a saucepan, add the rest of the ingredients and mix well.

*To make the second stuffing:* Sauté the onion in the butter, add the giblets and cook for 2 – 3 minutes. Add the rest of the ingredients and cook for a further 2 minutes, stirring well.

Make a paste with the lard, the minced Portuguese sausage, salt, pepper and paprika. Rub the turkey with the paste. Place some bacon strips across the turkey breast, wrap in tin foil (optional) and cook at 220° C for 50 minutes. Reduce the oven temperature to 180° C and continue cooking for 24 minutes per kg of turkey. Baste often with pan juices. When the turkey is cooked, remove it from the oven. Pour the Port wine over the turkey (to cool it), and return it to the oven for 5 – 10 minutes.

# Salads, Vegetables and Rice

## *Saladas, Legumes e Arroz*

Portuguese cooking does not do justice to the

beautiful and plentiful vegetables that are grown in

Portugal. Vegetables are mostly used in soups,

or are mashed or stewed in tons of tomato,

or used as fillers in some dish or other.

The end results are, nevertheless, delicious.

Many people are not aware that rice is grown

along the west coast of Portugal. It is a

short-grained rice, almost round, and very suitable

for Portuguese cooking (or was the cooking

adapted to the rice?). Rice is very popular, and is

sometimes served

with potatoes as well.

# Salads
## *Saladas*

# Algarve Salad
## *Salada Algarvia*

This is a very refreshing salad which should be prepared a few hours ahead of time so that the flavours blend. It is usually served with grilled sardines.

3 large green peppers
3 large tomatoes
1 onion, sliced

*Dressing*
1 clove garlic, crushed
salt and pepper
100 ml olive oil
30 ml vinegar
5 ml oregano

Place the peppers and tomatoes under the grill or over an open fire to char the skins. Remove the skins. De-pip the peppers and rinse. Cut the peppers into strips and chop the tomatoes roughly. Place in a bowl and add the sliced onion. Mix together the ingredients for the dressing and pour over the salad. Refrigerate for 2 – 3 hours.
**Serves 4 – 6.**

# Tomato and Cucumber Salad
## *Salada de Tomate e Pepino*

4 tomatoes, ripe but firm
1 cucumber
1 onion

*Dressing*
3 cloves garlic, chopped
10 ml oregano
30 ml olive oil
15 ml vinegar
salt and pepper to taste

Chop the tomatoes, cucumber and onion. Place in a salad bowl. Mix together the ingredients for the dressing and pour over the salad. Leave for 2 – 3 hours before serving.
**Serves 4 – 6.**

# Lettuce Salad
## *Salada de Alface*

In the Lisbon region lettuce salad is served with just about everything – hence the nickname given to the inhabitants: *alfacinhas*.

| | |
|---|---|
| lettuce (butter, red butter, oakleaf) | *Dressing* |
| | 25 ml olive oil |
| 1 onion, sliced | 10 ml vinegar |
| chopped coriander leaves | salt and pepper |
| | 2 cloves garlic, crushed |

Wash the lettuce well and drain. Place the ingredients for the salad dressing in a bowl with the coriander leaves. Beat with a fork. Add the lettuce and onion rings and toss. Add more dressing if necessary. Serve immediately.
   **Serves 4 – 6.**

**Variation**

Use watercress instead of lettuce *(Salada de Agrião)* and garnish with radishes.

# Green Bean Salad
## *Salada de Feijão Verde*

| | |
|---|---|
| 1 kg green beans | *Dressing* |
| hard-boiled eggs | 4 – 5 cloves garlic, crushed |
| 1 onion, sliced | 60 ml olive oil |
| 75 ml vinegar | 75 ml chopped coriander leaves |
| | *or* chopped parsley |
| | salt and pepper |

Top and tail the beans and cut in half lengthwise. Cook in boiling salted water until tender. Meanwhile mix together the ingredients for the dressing. Toss the onion rings in the dressing. Drain the beans well, toss in the dressing and leave to cool. Add the vinegar just before serving. Garnish with hard-boiled egg.
   **Serves 4 – 6.**

**Variation**

For a quick meal, many housewives add cubed boiled potatoes and a tin of sardines or tuna.

# Black-eyed Bean or Chick Pea Salad

## Salada de Feijão Frade ou Salada de Grão Bico

500 g black-eyed beans or
 chick peas
2 hard-boiled eggs, cut into
 wedges
10 olives
1 grilled green pepper

*Dressing*
30 ml olive oil
25 ml vinegar
15 ml chopped parsley
2 onions, chopped
salt and pepper

Soak the beans or chick peas overnight. Drain, cover with fresh water, and boil until soft. Drain and cool. Mix together the ingredients for the dressing. Place the beans or chick peas in a bowl, pour over the dressing and mix. Garnish with hard-boiled eggs, olives and green pepper strips.

Tinned chick peas and black-eyed beans are available and may be used.

**Serves 4 – 6.**

# Vegetables
## *Legumes*

# Potatoes
## *Batatas*

Potatoes *(batatas)* are known as *semilhas* in Madeira. Legend has it that the early inhabitants of the island gave them that name because the seed potatoes that went to Madeira and the Canary Islands had the word *semilla* (Spanish for 'seed') printed on the sacks. In Madeira the word *batata* is used for sweet potatoes. They are as sweet as honey and just as delicious. Try them baked, boiled, or thinly sliced and fried in hot oil.

As you have paged through this book (trying some of the recipes, I hope), you will have come across the recommendation 'serve with small fried potatoes' for just about everything. The Portuguese love their potatoes! We don't give them a chance to get old – the younger the better. Older potatoes are used for making chips, or for mashed potato which is also a great favourite. Egg yolks are often added to enrich mashed potatoes.

To break the monotony, I would like to share with you some of the ways in which I prepare potatoes – all of them with a Portuguese flavour.

# Boiled Potatoes
## *Batatas Cozidas*

8 – 10 medium potatoes (in
   their jackets)
salt and pepper
1 sprig of oregano
1 clove garlic, crushed
10 ml olive oil
piri piri (optional)

*Dressing*
2 cloves garlic, chopped
pepper
olive oil to taste

Slit the potatoes lengthwise. Place in a pan with the rest of the ingredients, cover with water and boil until cooked. Drain and peel the potatoes and cut in half. Add the chopped garlic and pepper, drizzle with olive oil and toss.

**Serves 4.**

**Variations**

Peel the cooked potatoes and brown in a frying pan with one of the following:

* Oil, butter and freshly chopped coriander or mint leaves.
* Oil, butter, bay leaves and garlic.
* Oil, butter, piri piri, ground cumin and paprika.

# Spicy Potatoes
## *Batatas Picantes*

| | |
|---|---|
| 8 – 10 medium potatoes | 5 ml each of ground coriander, |
| 2 medium onions, chopped | ground cumin, mustard seed, |
| 10 ml olive oil | turmeric, ground fennel |
| 20 g butter | fresh coriander leaves |

Leave the potatoes in their jackets. Slit them lengthwise, place in a saucepan, cover with water and boil until soft. Drain and peel the potatoes and cut them into cubes.

Sauté the onion in the oil and butter until soft but not brown. Add the spices, stir well and cook for a couple of minutes. Add the cubed potatoes and stir lightly so as not to break them. Sprinkle with chopped coriander leaves and serve.

**Serves 4.**

# Roast Potatoes
## *Batatas no Forno*

| | |
|---|---|
| 1 kg small potatoes | 5 ml ground cumin |
| 100 g butter, melted | salt and pepper |
| 10 ml olive oil | piri piri to taste |
| 10 ml paprika | 5 ml instant chicken stock |
| | powder |

Allow 5 – 6 potatoes per person. Peel the potatoes, or leave them in their jackets, and parboil. Drain the potatoes and place them in a roasting dish. Place the remaining ingredients in a bowl and either microwave on full power for 2 minutes or melt in a small saucepan. Pour the butter mixture over the potatoes, toss and bake at 180° C for 25 – 30 minutes.

I doubt if you will have any left over, but if you do, use them in a (spicy) potato salad.

**Serves 4.**

# Grandpa's Potatoes
## *Batatas do Avôzinho*

Another of my grandfather's specialities. When we were children this dish was often served to us as a meal. Today I omit the eggs and serve it as an accompaniment to meat or fish dishes that are on the 'dry' side.

15 ml olive oil
20 g butter
500 g onions, sliced
1 kg potatoes, thinly sliced

salt and pepper
3 – 4 eggs (optional)
fresh oregano

Place a little oil and butter in a large frying pan. Place layers of onion and potato in the oil, sprinkling with salt and pepper between each layer. Cover and cook gently without stirring for 30 – 35 minutes or until the vegetables are cooked. A lovely crust forms at the bottom of the pan – we used to fight over it!

Beat the eggs with the oregano, pour over the potatoes, cover and cook until the eggs are set.

**Serves 4 – 6.**


# Baked Potatoes
## *Batatas à Murro*

Can be baked in the oven or in hot coals.

500 g medium potatoes in their jackets
25 ml coarse salt
2 cloves garlic, crushed
20 ml olive oil

*Oven-baked:* Sprinkle half the salt on a baking tray. Place the potatoes on the salt and sprinkle the rest of the salt over them. Bake at 180° C for approximately 40 minutes.

*Or:* Sprinkle the potatoes with the salt. Wrap them in foil and nestle them in amongst the coals for 45 minutes. When they are baked, shake off the excess salt and hit them with your fist to squash them *(murro!).*

Heat the garlic in the olive oil and drizzle the oil over the potatoes just before serving.

**Serves 4 – 6.**

# Salty Potatoes
## *Batatas Apertadas de Sal*

Do not let the amount of salt put you off. The result is amazing. The potatoes are not salty but acquire almost a seafood taste. The potatoes must have a thick skin (middle-aged potatoes). Do not remove the eyes and if possible have them all more or less the same size.

    1 kg medium potatoes
    350 ml coarse salt
    1 litre hot water

Wash the potatoes. Dissolve the salt in the hot water and add the potatoes – the water should just cover the potatoes. Boil until all the liquid has evaporated and the potatoes are cooked. The potatoes will be covered in a white powder. Shake it off and serve immediately.
**Serves 4.**

# Chou-Chou or Chayote
## *Pimpinelas*

Chou-chou is a member of the squash family. It is pear-shaped and light green or pale yellow (almost white) in colour. It is grown and used extensively in Madeira and can be obtained locally during the summer months. Try and grow your own – it is a beautiful creeper. The 'elders' say that it controls cholesterol levels.

    Chou-chou are at their best when medium-sized with a thin skin. Older ones can be added to soups and stews. Small chou-chou (the size of patty pans) are delicious just boiled and served with a butter sauce. (Not Portuguese? Why not?)

3 – 4 chou-chou
salt and pepper
1 sprig of oregano
1 clove garlic, crushed
10 ml olive oil
piri piri (optional)

*Dressing*
2 cloves garlic, chopped
pepper
olive oil to taste

Cut the chou-chou in half and leave in water for 30 minutes. Scrape off any stickiness. Chou-chou may be cooked with or without their skins. Place in a pan with the rest of the ingredients, cover with water and boil until soft. Drain, add chopped garlic and pepper, drizzle with olive oil and toss. Chou-chou may be cooked separately or together with potatoes.

**Serves 4 – 6.**

**Variations**

✳ Boil the chou-chou as described above. Drain, peel and slice and place in an ovenproof dish. Pour a rich cheese sauce over the chou-chou and brown under the grill.

✳ Chou-chou stewed with olive oil, tomatoes, onion, garlic and piri piri makes a delicious vegetarian dish.

# Yam
## *Inhame*

This vegetable is best known to South African greengrocers by its Zulu name, *Madumbi*. It is a tuber which is very similar to the sweet potato. Peel and soak it in water for 1 – 2 hours – it is very sticky. *Madumbi* can be boiled by itself for 45 minutes to 1 hour, or cooked with potatoes, sweet potatoes, green beans or mealies.

# Green Beans
## *Feijão Verde (Vagem ou Vaginha)*

Green beans must be second in line to the vegetable 'throne' (potatoes are indisputably first). No matter how small the garden, the Portuguese will always find room for bean vines. They are boiled, stewed, added to soups and served in many interesting ways – such as *Peixinhos de Horta* (no, it does not contain fish).

# Garden Fish
## *Peixinhos de Horta*

500 g green beans
salt and pepper
lemon juice
oil for frying

*Batter*
125 g flour
salt and pepper
2 eggs
100 ml water
100 ml white wine or beer

Cut the beans in half (make them equal lengths) and boil them, uncovered, in salted water until tender. Season with pepper and lemon juice.

Meanwhile, make the batter. Sift the flour into a bowl. Season with salt and pepper. Make a well in the centre and add the eggs, water and wine or beer. Mix well into a thin batter. Thread the cooked and drained beans on to toothpicks, dip in the batter and fry in hot oil. Drain. Remove the toothpicks and serve.

**Serves 4 – 6.**

# Stewed Beans
## *Feijão Guisado*

1 kg green beans
20 ml olive oil
10 ml butter
2 onions, chopped

1 bay leaf
3 tomatoes, grated
10 ml vinegar
sprig of fresh herbs

Wash and cut the beans lengthwise into long slices. Sauté the onion and bay leaf in the olive oil and butter. Add the tomatoes and simmer for 10 minutes until thick. Add the green beans and a little water if necessary. Add the vinegar and herbs and simmer until the beans are cooked.

**Serves 4 – 6.**

**Variation**
Substitute slices of young turnip for the beans.

# Sprouts
## Grelos (Espigos)

Flowering sprouts or young shoots of any kind may be used . . . broccoli, cabbage, turnips. They can also be added to stews, soups and rice.

> 1 bunch sprouts
> 150 ml olive oil
> 3 cloves garlic, crushed
> salt and pepper

Cook the sprouts in salted water for 5 – 10 minutes. Drain well and chop. Heat the oil and the garlic in a frying pan, add the sprouts, mix well, season with salt and pepper and serve immediately.
**Serves 4 – 6.**

# Sautéd Spinach
## Esparregado

In Portugal tender turnip leaves (nabiças) are used for this dish (I told you we use everything!) but young spinach leaves may also be used. A combination of the two is delicious.

> 2 bunches spinach leaves          salt and pepper
> 50 ml olive oil                          15 ml flour
> 1 bay leaf                                 5 ml vinegar
> 4 cloves garlic, whole              sprinkling of nutmeg

Cook the spinach until it is tender. Drain well and slice. Heat the olive oil and the bay leaf. Add the garlic and fry until it is golden. Remove the garlic and the bay leaf. Add the chopped spinach to the hot oil, season with salt and pepper and stir for 1 – 2 minutes. Add the flour and stir to absorb any liquid. Lastly, add the vinegar and nutmeg.
**Serves 4 – 6.**

# Stewed Peas
## *Ervilhas com Ovos*

1 *chouriço*, sliced
1 onion, chopped
1 clove garlic, chopped
coriander leaves, chopped
10 ml olive oil
500 g peas

salt and pepper
sprinkling of sugar
spring onion tops
125 ml water
4 eggs

Sauté the *chouriço*, onion, garlic and coriander leaves in the olive oil. Add the peas and stir well. Add the salt, pepper and sugar. Sprinkle the onion tops over the peas, add the water and simmer until cooked. Poach the eggs in the peas. In some regions a chopped tomato is added to the *chouriço*, onion, etc.
**Serves 4.**

# Portuguese Broad Beans
## *Favas à Portuguesa*

4 kg broad beans
150 g bacon, chopped
150 g blood sausage, sliced
  (optional)
150 g *chouriço*, sliced
20 ml olive oil

1 onion, chopped
3 cloves garlic, crushed
10 ml paprika
salt and pepper
coriander leaves

Shell the beans and remove the 'eyes'. Fry the meats in the olive oil, add the onion, garlic, beans, paprika and salt and pepper. Stir well. Add just enough water to cover and simmer until cooked. Drain. Sprinkle with chopped coriander leaves and serve with a lettuce salad.
**Serves 4 – 6.**

# Beans with Cabbage
## Feijão com Couve

In the Santarém region this is a very popular accompaniment to grilled sardines.

250 g sugar beans, soaked
   overnight
1 small onion
salt

10 ml olive oil
500 ml coarsely shredded kale
   leaves
1 *broa* (see p152)

Drain the beans, cover with fresh water, and boil with the onion, salt and olive oil until they are tender. Strain. Boil the cabbage in salted water and strain when cooked. Mix the cabbage and the beans together. Place some cubes of bread in individual soup bowls. Ladle the beans and cabbage over the bread and serve with grilled sardines. (The water used to cook the beans and cabbage can be used for soup.)
   **Serves 4.**

# Stewed Cabbage with Purslane
## Couves com Beldroegas (Baldroegas)

Perhaps you don't know what purslane is? It is a low-growing succulent salad herb which probably grows wild in your garden and you weed it out and throw it away. In Portugal purslane is cultivated specially for use in salads, soups and stews and is sold just like any other herb or vegetable. The cultivated variety has large tender leaves. It makes a most delicious soup and definitely adds something to a stew.

1 onion, chopped
2 cloves garlic, pressed
15 ml olive oil
50 g *chouriço*, finely chopped
2 tomatoes, grated

salt and piri piri to taste
1 bay leaf
1 sugarloaf cabbage, finely
   chopped
1 potato, peeled and cubed
250 ml chopped purslane

Sauté the onion and garlic in the olive oil, add the *chouriço* and cook for a few minutes. Add the tomatoes, seasonings and bay leaf and simmer until thick. Add the chopped cabbage, the cubed potato and the purslane. Simmer until the vegetables are tender.

When I have the time (which is not very often), I stew all the ingredients except the cabbage until the mixture is thick and then stuff blanched cabbage leaves with it. The stuffed cabbage leaves are then simmered in a tomato and onion mixture (*refogado*, see p120) until cooked.

**Serves 4 – 6.**

# Braised Onions
## *Cebolas Estufadas*

Ideal as an accompaniment to game and poultry dishes.

| | |
|---|---|
| 1 kg medium onions | piri piri to taste |
| 75 ml olive oil | 2 ml paprika |
| 25 ml butter | 350 ml chicken stock |
| 1 carrot, diced | salt, if necessary |
| 1 bay leaf | chopped parsley |

Peel the onions, just the outer layer, from the root end. Do not cut the top off – this will keep the onion whole.

In a deep frying pan with a lid, sauté the carrot in the oil and butter. Add the bay leaf, piri piri and paprika. Add the onions and brown them, turning them constantly and carefully. Add the stock, check the seasoning, cover and simmer until the onions are tender. Add more stock if necessary. Garnish with chopped parsley.

**Serves 4 – 6.**

# Braised Fennel
## *Funcho Estufado*

| | |
|---|---|
| 6 fennel bulbs | 1 bay leaf |
| 125 g bacon, diced | 2 onions, sliced |
| 2 cloves garlic, crushed | 1 carrot, sliced |
| 15 ml olive oil | 250 ml chicken stock |
| 150 ml tomato, grated | 25 ml white wine |
| 5 ml paprika | 15 ml Port wine |

Clean the fennel bulbs and cut each in half. Soak in salted water for 30 minutes. Rinse and parboil for 10 minutes.

Sauté the bacon and garlic in the olive oil. Add the tomato, paprika and bay leaf and simmer until thick. Place some of the bacon mixture in a flameproof casserole dish, followed by a layer of sliced onions and carrot. Add the fennel halves and repeat the layers of bacon and vegetables, ending with a layer of onion.

Mix the stock and the wines in a jug and pour over the contents of the casserole. Cover and simmer for 10 minutes. Drain the sauce back into the jug. Taste the sauce and adjust the seasonings. Pour it back into the casserole and simmer until the fennel is cooked. (This dish may also be baked in the oven at 180° C for 30 – 35 minutes.)

**Serves 4 – 6.**

# Sintra Carrots
## *Cenouras à Moda de Sintra*

500 g sweet baby carrots
half a chicken stock cube *or*
   5 ml instant chicken stock
   powder, mixed with 250 ml
   water
15 ml butter

15 ml flour
3 egg yolks
salt and pepper
5 ml chopped mint
5 ml chopped parsley

Wash the carrots and boil them in the chicken stock until they are tender. Strain and reserve the stock. In a saucepan, melt the butter, add the flour, stir well and cook for 1 – 2 minutes. Add the stock slowly, stirring until thick. Mix the egg yolks with a little of the hot sauce and then stir into the rest of the sauce. Season with salt and pepper. Simmer gently for 2 – 3 minutes until the egg is cooked – do not boil. Add the carrots, chopped mint and parsley. Stir gently and serve.

**Serves 4 – 6.**

# Baked Pumpkin
## *Frade Assado*

*Frade* is a special pumpkin grown mainly in the Alentejo and Algarve provinces. I use butternut or a very ripe pumpkin.

| | |
|---|---|
| 150 g bacon, diced | salt and pepper |
| 2 – 3 cloves garlic, crushed | 5 ml paprika |
| 3 onions, chopped | 100 ml beef stock |
| 1 bay leaf | 100 ml wine |
| 2 tomatoes, grated | 1,5 kg pumpkin, cut into slices |
| 10 ml olive oil | 10 ml flour |

Sauté the bacon, garlic, onions, bay leaf and tomatoes in the olive oil. Season to taste with the salt, pepper and paprika. Add the stock and the wine and simmer until thick. Place the pumpkin in a roasting pan and pour the sauce over it. Dust with flour and bake at 180° C for 40 – 45 minutes, or until the pumpkin is cooked.

If the bacon is omitted, this is a delicious vegetarian dish.

**Serves 4 – 6.**

# Rice
## *Arroz*

# Party Rice
## *Arroz à Valenciana*

This dish is a must at all Portuguese parties. My friend Maria do Carmo makes the best *Arroz à Valenciana* in the world. To her, preparing rice for 200 people is as easy as falling off a log. (No, she does not offer a catering service – she cooks only for friends and family. So you have the choice of either becoming her friend very quickly, or trying this recipe, which I have simplified slightly.)

| | |
|---|---|
| 200 g lean pork | salt, pepper and piri piri to taste |
| 200 g steak | 5 ml turmeric |
| 125 g veal | 1 small chicken, cut into pieces |
| 50 g *presunto* (bacon may be substituted) | 500 g seafood mix |
| 125 ml olive oil | 100 g prawns, deveined |
| 100 g butter | 500 g rice |
| 2 large onions, chopped | water or chicken stock |
| 1 *chouriço*, sliced | 250 g frozen peas |
| | 250 g frozen carrots |

3 green peppers, chopped
1 sprig of parsley
750 ml grated tomatoes

6 Vienna sausages, sliced
1 large tin mussels

Cut the meats and the *presunto* into cubes. Place in a very large pot with the olive oil and butter and fry until brown. Add the onions and *chouriço* and continue frying until they are brown. Add the peppers, parsley, tomato, seasoning and turmeric and simmer until the meats are nearly cooked. Add the chicken pieces, the seafood mix, prawns and rice and stir well. Add enough water or chicken stock to cook the rice and simmer until the rice is tender. Add the peas, carrots and Viennas. Stir and cook for 5 minutes. Gently stir in the mussels just before serving.

Serve straight from the pot.

**Serves 10 – 12.**

**Variation**

Some recipes use rabbit and eel as well.

# Buttered Rice
## *Arroz de Manteiga*

Whenever 'plain rice' is mentioned in a recipe it refers to *arroz de manteiga*. In most restaurants, and even at home, plain rice is served moulded (that is, placed inside a cup and then turned out before serving). I suppose the attractive shape makes up for its being plain rice. When rice is cooked in salted water only it is called *arroz à crioula* or *arroz à indiana*.

50 g butter
1 clove garlic, whole
1 bay leaf
500 ml rice

1 litre water
1 onion
2 cloves
salt and pepper

Melt 25 ml of the butter in a pot. Sauté the garlic and the bay leaf in the butter and then remove them. Add the rice, mixing it well with the butter. Add the water. Stick the cloves into the onion and place it in the pot with the rice. Cover and simmer until the rice is cooked. Remove the onion. Add the remaining butter, season, and fluff the rice with a fork. Mould the rice, or serve it as it is.

**Serves 4 – 6.**

**Variations**

\* Add cooked peas or grated carrots to the rice.

\* For spicy rice, add 1 cinnamon stick, 1 ml ground cinnamon, 5 ml paprika, 2 allspice and 1 clove to the butter in the pan, together with the garlic and bay leaf.

# Rice with Sprouts
## *Arroz de Grelos*

2 large onions, chopped
3 cloves garlic, crushed
100 ml olive oil
1 bunch flowering sprouts

500 ml rice
salt and pepper
1 litre water

Sauté the onions and garlic in the oil. Add the washed sprouts (whole) and sauté. Add the rice. Stir well, and add the seasoning and water. Cook until the rice is tender – 15 – 20 minutes. If a 'looser' rice is required, use 750 ml water to 250 ml rice.

**Serves 4 – 6.**

# Tomato Rice
## *Arroz de Tomate*

Tomato Rice is a hot favourite with the Portuguese. Unfortunately my grand-mother did not pass on to me her secret for this recipe – no one has ever been able to make it the way she did. Was it perhaps the earthenware casserole she used, or the full flavour of very ripe tomatoes, or the fat *(toucinho)*?

2 onions, chopped
1 clove garlic, chopped
25 ml olive oil
20 g lard (optional)
4 ripe tomatoes, grated
1 green pepper, chopped
    (optional)

1 bay leaf
salt and pepper
500 ml rice
1 litre chicken, beef or vegetable
    stock (depending on what you
    are serving with the rice)

Sauté the onions and garlic in the oil and lard. Add the tomatoes, green pepper, bay leaf and seasoning and simmer until thick. Add the rice, stirring well. Add the stock, cover, and simmer until the rice is cooked. Broccoli or peas may be added 10 minutes before the rice is served.

**Serves 4.**

# Rice with Beans
## *Feijão com Arroz*

When we were children we were always allowed to choose a favourite dish for a birthday treat. I loved rice with beans (funnily enough, my children do too), so this was my treat. Everyone else seemed to have far more lavish birthday dishes, while I was stuck with beans. In the end I decided that I hated rice with beans . . . but only so that my birthdays could be a little more exciting.

| | |
|---|---|
| 500 g sugar beans | 2 cloves garlic, whole |
| 250 g pork rib (spare-ribs) | 1 onion, chopped |
| 100 g *chouriço* | 500 ml rice |
| 10 ml olive oil | 10 ml paprika |
| 1 bay leaf | salt and pepper to taste |

Soak the beans overnight. Drain, place in a large saucepan and cover with fresh water. Add all the remaining ingredients except the rice and seasoning. Bring to the boil and cook until the beans are tender. Add the rice, paprika and seasoning and simmer until the rice is done.

This is a lovely dish for a winter brunch. If you are serving it as an accompaniment to a meat or fish dish, omit the pork rib and *chouriço.*

**Serves 4 – 6.**

# Rice Croquettes
## *Croquetes de Arroz*

| | |
|---|---|
| 200 g white rice | 15 ml grated cheese |
| 450 ml water | salt and pepper |
| 125 ml *chouriço* or ham, | 25 ml flour |
| very finely chopped | breadcrumbs |
| 2 eggs, separated | cooking oil for frying |
| 10 ml chopped fresh herbs | |

Boil the rice in salted water until it is very soft – it should resemble thick porridge. Add the *chouriço,* the egg yolks, herbs, grated cheese and seasoning. Place in the refrigerator until cold. Mould into croquettes, roll in flour, dip in the beaten egg whites, and roll in breadcrumbs. Reshape. Place on a tray lined with kitchen paper and refrigerate for 15 – 20 minutes. Fry in deep oil.

**Serves 4 – 6.**

**Variation**
Rice croquettes can be served as an accompaniment to meat and fish dishes, or as a light meal with a salad. If you plan to serve them as a meal, try placing 2 – 5 ml cooked beef mince inside each croquette before rolling.

# Seafood Rice
## *Arroz de Marisco*

1 onion, chopped
45 ml olive oil
4 tomatoes, chopped *or*
   1 tin whole tomatoes
2 – 3 cloves garlic, crushed
1 sprig of parsley
1 bay leaf
10 ml paprika

1 green pepper, chopped
salt and pepper
500 g seafood mix
500 ml rice
1 litre water
3 large prawns, deveined
1 tin mussels in shells
  (optional)
coriander leaves

Fry the onion in the olive oil. Add the tomatoes, garlic, parsley, bay leaf, paprika, green pepper, salt and pepper. Cook for a few seconds and then add the seafood mix and the rice. Stir well. Add the water and bring to the boil. Simmer until the rice is tender (about 20 minutes). Add the prawns. Gently stir the mussels into the rice just before serving.

Serve on a large platter, garnished with whole prawns and chopped coriander leaves.

**Serves 6 – 8.**

**Variation**
For an extra special touch, add some crab claws when you add the prawns.

# Dried Cod Rice
## *Arroz de Bacalhau*

250 g *bacalhau*
100 ml olive oil
2 onions, chopped
1 clove garlic, chopped
10 ml chopped parsley
1 bay leaf

3 ripe tomatoes, chopped
1 green pepper, chopped
salt and pepper
5 ml paprika
500 ml rice
1 litre water

Soak the dried fish for 24 hours. Drain, wash and dry with kitchen paper. Fry the onions in the olive oil. Add the garlic, parsley, bay leaf, tomatoes, green pepper and flaked fish. Season with the salt, pepper and paprika and cook for 5 minutes. Add the rice, stirring well. Add the water, cover and simmer until the rice is cooked. Serve with a green salad.

(Although not typically Portuguese, toasted flaked almonds sprinkled over the rice just before serving add a delicious extra touch.)

**Serves 4.**

# Octopus Rice
## *Arroz de Polvo*

100 ml olive oil
2 onions, chopped
2 cloves garlic, crushed
1 bay leaf
1 sprig of parsley
10 ml paprika

salt and pepper
1 octopus (prepared as
    described on p6)
250 ml rice
750 ml water

Place the oil in a pot and fry the onion and garlic. Add the bay leaf, parsley, paprika and salt and pepper to taste. Add the octopus and cook for about 30 minutes. Add the rice and water, cover, and simmer until the rice is tender. This dish is on the 'watery' side – more like a thick soup.

**Serves 4 – 6.**

# Rice with Limpets
## *Arroz de Lapas*

Remember that limpets are protected. Ask your local department of environmental affairs for details before you start collecting.

| | |
|---|---|
| 1 kg small limpets | 1 ml ground cumin |
| boiling water | 1 ml curry powder |
| 60 ml olive oil | white pepper |
| 1 onion, chopped | 2 cloves |
| 2 cloves garlic, crushed | 1 sprig of parsley |
| 1 tomato, grated | 500 ml rice |
| 1 bay leaf | 20 ml Madeira wine |
| 2 ml paprika | coriander leaves |

Wash the limpets and soak in salted water for 30 minutes. Rinse. Pour boiling water over the limpets. Remove from the shells. Strain the liquid and reserve.

Make a *refogado,* using the olive oil, onion, garlic and tomato (see p120), and add the bay leaf, spices and parsley. Add the rice and 1,5 litres of liquid made up from fresh water and the liquid reserved after straining the limpets. Just before serving gently stir in the limpets and the Madeira wine and check the seasoning. Sprinkle with chopped coriander leaves.

**Serves 4 – 6.**

## Other Grain Dishes

# Couscous
## *Cuscus*

Couscous is of Moroccan origin. It is still home-made in Madeira today, but ready-made imported couscous can be bought locally. Although the ingredients for home-made couscous are simple, the recipe is so unendingly complicated that one cannot help but be grateful for the ready-made product which can be prepared very quickly. Couscous is a very useful substitute for potatoes and can be served as an accompaniment to many dishes.

50 g butter (herb or garlic
    butter can be used)
1 sprig of thyme
1 clove garlic, whole

250 g couscous
5 ml salt
250 ml water

Melt the butter in a saucepan and add the thyme and the garlic. Fry for 1 – 2 minutes. Remove the garlic, add the couscous and salt and stir with a fork. Pour on the water. Bring to the boil and simmer for 5 minutes. Cover the pan and allow to stand for 15 – 20 minutes before serving.

**Serves 4 – 6.**

# 'More-ish' Couscous
## *Mais e Mais Cuscus*

Although this is not a typically Portuguese dish, the ingredients have such a strong Portuguese character that whenever I make the dish people always ask for more.

500 g chick peas, soaked
    and cooked
500 g couscous, cooked
    as described above
250 g green beans, sliced
    and cooked
250 g cooked carrots, cubed
1 green pepper, blanched
    and sliced
8 – 10 black olives, pitted

*Dressing*
125 ml olive oil
5 – 6 cloves garlic
half a bunch of coriander leaves
15 ml lemon juice
1 ml ground cumin
1 ml ground cinnamon
salt and pepper

*Garnish*
onion rings
cherry tomatoes
coriander leaves

Mix the chick peas, couscous and vegetables together in a large bowl. Place all the ingredients for the dressing in a blender and blend for 1 – 2 minutes. Pour the dressing over the ingredients in the bowl and mix using 2 large forks. Garnish with onion rings, cherry tomatoes and chopped coriander leaves.

**Serves 8 – 10.**

# Cooked Mealie Meal
## *Milho Cozido*

Traditionally served in Madeira to accompany fish dishes.

| | |
|---|---|
| 2,5 litres water | 1 sprig of thyme |
| 10 ml olive oil | 500 g mealie meal |
| 25 ml butter | chopped parsley *or* chopped |
| salt | cabbage leaves (optional) |
| 3 cloves garlic, whole | |

Place the water, oil, butter, salt, garlic and thyme in a large pot and bring to the boil. Mix the mealie meal with enough cold water to form a paste. Add the paste very carefully to the boiling water in the pot. Whisk briskly. Reduce the heat and simmer for about 1 hour, stirring occasionally. Add the parsley or cabbage leaves just before serving.

**Serves 4 – 6**.

# Fried Mealie Meal
## *Milho Frito*

Cook the mealie meal as described above. Pour it into a rectangular dish and cool. Refrigerate overnight. Next day cut the mealie meal into cubes and fry in oil. Before turning the cubes, make sure that a crust has formed. Serve with fish or meat.

For a sweet treat, cook the mealie meal in salt and water only. Pour honey over the fried cubes.

# Mealie Meal with Sardines
## *Papas de Milho com Sardinhas*

In the Algarve yellow mealie meal is used. Small sardines or clams are often added to it. It is served either as a meal on its own or as an accompaniment to fried or grilled fish.

300 g sardines
25 ml olive oil
2 small onions, chopped
1 tomato, grated
1 sprig of parsley *or* coriander

salt and pepper
5 ml vinegar
2,5 litres water
500 g mealie meal

Clean and gut the sardines. Cut them in half and sprinkle with salt.

Heat the oil and fry the onions. Add the tomato, parsley, salt and pepper and simmer for 5 – 10 minutes. Add the sardines and cook for a further 5 minutes. Add the vinegar. Remove the sardines from the broth and keep to one side. Pour the broth and the 2,5 litres water into a large pot. Add the mealie meal, which has first been mixed to a paste with a little cold water, and whisk briskly. Cook for 40 – 45 minutes, stirring occasionally. (The mixture should be the consistency of thick cream – add more water if it becomes dry.)

Add half the sardines and mix lightly. Serve the rest of the sardines separately.

**Serves 4 – 6.**

# Sauces, Dressings and Flavourings
## *Molhos e Temperos*

If you should happen to walk into a Portuguese

kitchen when a meal is in the initial stages of

preparation, you will encounter a very characteristic

aroma. All that is happening is that onions are being

fried in olive oil with garlic . . . and this is called

*refogado.* Tomatoes, green peppers and seasonings

may be added, according to the requirements

of the particular recipe, and the sauce may be

strained or sieved.

# Tomato Sauce
## *Tomatada*

Tomato Sauce is used in stews, ladled over fried fish, or as a basis for rice and other dishes.

| | |
|---|---|
| 50 ml olive oil | 10 ml chopped parsley |
| 3 large onions, chopped | 10 ml paprika |
| 1 clove garlic, chopped | 1 ml ground cumin |
| 500 ml tomato, grated | 2 cloves |
| 1 bay leaf | 3 peppercorns |

Make a *refogado* . . . You would start by frying the onions and garlic in the oil. Add all the remaining ingredients and simmer until thick. Sometimes a little wine is added . . . depends on whether you have any to spare for cooking . . .

# Piri Piri Sauce
## *Molho de Piri Piri*

There are dozens of recipes for piri piri sauce. I prefer this very simple one.

Piri piri chillies are *very* hot. Unless you grow your own, they may be bought as dried, whole chillies. If you are using fresh chillies, crush or slice them, place them in a jar or bottle (preferably one with a cork top), add 2 cloves of crushed garlic, a small piece of lemon rind, 5 ml lemon juice and 5 ml salt. Fill the rest of the bottle with two-thirds mixed olive and cooking oil and one-third vinegar. Cork the bottle and shake once a day. Leave for at least 10 – 15 days before using.

For a quicker version, boil the juice of 2 lemons with 100 ml dried piri piri for 2 minutes. Strain. Crush the chillies with 5 ml salt and 2 cloves of crushed garlic. Add to the strained liquid and store.

# Madeira Wine Sauce
## *Molho Para Carne*

This sauce is suitable for serving with sliced tongue or sliced braised beef
(*Carne Estufada*).

| | |
|---|---|
| 75 g butter | 500 ml beef stock |
| 100 g bacon, diced | 125 ml red wine |
| 2 carrots, diced | peppercorns to taste |
| 1 onion, chopped | 25 ml tomato paste |
| 2 cloves garlic, crushed | 10 ml chopped parsley |
| 1 stick celery, chopped | salt and pepper to taste |
| 25 ml flour | 50 ml Madeira *or* Port wine |

Melt the butter. Add the bacon, carrots, onion, garlic and celery and sauté
until soft. Add the flour and stir until brown. Add the stock, red wine, peppercorns, tomato paste, chopped parsley and seasoning. Simmer for about 1 hour.
Strain. Add the Madeira or Port wine to the strained sauce and adjust the
seasoning. Bring to the boil and use as required.

# White Sauce
## *Molho Béchamel*

The quantities given below make 500 ml sauce.

| | |
|---|---|
| 1 onion | 6 – 8 peppercorns |
| 4 cloves | 1 bay leaf |
| 500 ml milk | 50 g butter |
| 1 carrot | 75 ml flour |
| 1 small stick cinnamon | salt and pepper |
| 1 stick celery | |

Stick the cloves into the onion. Place it in a saucepan with the milk, carrot,
cinnamon, celery, peppercorns and bay leaf and bring slowly to the boil.
Remove from the heat, cover and leave for 30 minutes. Strain.

Melt the butter. Add the flour and cook for 1 – 2 minutes, forming a 'roux'.
Remove from the heat and add the milk slowly to the roux using a whisk to
stir. Return to the heat and, whisking all the time, cook until thick. Season with
salt and pepper.

**Variations**

∗ Not all recipes require that you 'infuse' the milk with the onion, cloves, carrot, cinnamon stick, etc. This step can also be omitted if you are in a hurry.

∗ If a thicker sauce is required (eg for Meat Croquettes, p7), less liquid is used.

∗ For a richer sauce (eg for Prawn Patties, p4), 1 or more egg yolks may be added after the sauce has thickened.

∗ Different flavourings (mustard, chopped parsley, grated cheese) may be required for different recipes. These should be added after the sauce has thickened.

# Vinaigrette Sauce
## *Molho de Vinagre*

This sauce is suitable for all grilled and boiled fish dishes.

| | |
|---|---|
| 250 ml olive oil | chopped parsley *or* coriander |
| 75 ml wine vinegar | leaves *or* both |
| 4 – 5 cloves garlic, crushed | salt and pepper *or* piri piri |
| or pressed | |

Mix all the ingredients together just before required. Some dishes require lemon juice in addition to, or instead of, the vinegar.

# Country Sauce
## *Molho de Vilão*

This is a very good substitute for mayonnaise and is served mostly with fish.

| | |
|---|---|
| 200 ml olive oil | 50 ml chopped parsley *or* |
| 75 ml vinegar | coriander leaves |
| 1 onion, chopped | 1 clove garlic |
| 3 hard-boiled eggs, chopped | salt and pepper |

Mix the oil and vinegar together in a bowl. In a separate bowl mix all the remaining ingredients together into a paste. Add the vinegar and oil mixture slowly to the paste, beating all the time. Taste and adjust seasoning if necessary.

# Escabeche

*Escabeche* means 'vinegar sauce'. Different regions in Portugal have different versions of this sauce. In the Algarve it is made to accompany fried fish, especially left-over fish which it heats and moistens. The sauce can be made with the oil that remains after frying fish, but it should be strained before use.

15 ml olive oil
3 large onions, sliced
3 cloves garlic, crushed
5 ml paprika
salt and pepper

piri piri (optional)
1 bay leaf
10 ml chopped parsley
75 ml vinegar

Sauté the onions and garlic in the oil until soft but not brown. Add the paprika, salt, pepper, piri piri, bay leaf and chopped parsley. Simmer for 2 – 3 minutes. Add the vinegar, bring to the boil and pour over the fish.

# *Escabeche* Madeira-style

This is more of a pickling sauce, used for onions, tuna, etc.

125 ml cider vinegar
125 ml wine vinegar
350 ml olive oil
1 bay leaf
6 cloves garlic, crushed

salt
5 allspice
3 cloves
10 ml paprika

Mix all the ingredients together and use as required.

# Portuguese Salad Dressing
## *Tempero Para Salada*

I usually make this dressing in large quantities, especially in the summer, and store it in the refrigerator.

| | |
|---|---|
| 6 cloves garlic, whole | pepper |
| 250 ml olive oil | one of the following: coriander |
| 100 ml wine vinegar | leaves, oregano, thyme |
| 5 ml salt | |

Place all the ingredients together in a large jar. Close and shake well. Store in the refrigerator, using as required.

# Garlic Butter

| | |
|---|---|
| 250 g butter | 8 – 10 cloves garlic, crushed |
| 20 ml lemon juice | 25 ml chopped coriander leaves |
| 5 ml salt | piri piri to taste |

Cream the butter. Add the remaining ingredients and mix well. (A food processor works wonders.) Turn on to aluminium foil, shape into a roll, wrap and reshape. Keep in the refrigerator or freeze (don't forget to label it!).

**Variation**
*Herb Butter:* Add chopped fresh herbs (thyme, oregano) and proceed as above.

*Clockwise from the left*
Algarve Salad; *Bacalhau* before soaking; Chick Pea Salad;
Black-eyed Bean Salad; Fresh Sardines; Charcoal Grilled Sardines;
Charcoal Grilled Cod

*Clockwise from the left*
Rice Pudding; Portuguese Crème Caramel (before cooking);
Portuguese Dreams

# Coconut Milk
## *Leite de Coco*

Bottled coconut milk is sometimes available but if you can't find it, you can make your own.

1 coconut
185 ml milk
500 ml hot water

Make holes at one end of the coconut and drain the liquid (*água de coco*, coconut water) into a small jug. Place the whole coconut in a hot oven for 20 minutes. Break the coconut shell with a hammer. Remove the brown skin from the white coconut flesh with a vegetable peeler. Place the coconut flesh in a food processor with the coconut water (save a little of the latter to add to your favourite whisky) and blend. Place the blended coconut in a saucepan with the milk and heat, but do not boil. Remove from the heat, allow to stand for 10 minutes and then pour into a sieve. Press the pulp with the back of a spoon to extract as much milk as possible from the coconut pulp. Pour the hot water over the coconut in the sieve and allow it to drip through the coconut pulp. Bottle the coconut milk and store it in the refrigerator.

# Confectioner's Custard
## *Creme de Pasteleiro*

Confectioner's Custard is used as a filling for cakes and tarts.

4 egg yolks
2 whole eggs
150 g sugar
30 ml flour

15 ml cornflour (maizena)
500 ml milk
1 vanilla pod
15 ml butter

Beat the egg yolks and the whole eggs with the sugar until fluffy. Stir in the flour and maizena to form a paste. Heat the milk with the vanilla pod. Discard the vanilla pod and slowly pour the milk over the paste, mixing well. Return the mixture to the saucepan and bring to the boil, stirring all the time. Continue cooking until the mixture is thick. Add the butter and beat well.

For a lighter custard, beaten cream may be added when cool.

# Desserts and Sweets
## *Sobremesas e Doces*

Fresh fruit is a popular ending for a Portuguese

meal. Desserts are reserved mainly for special

occasions and many of them have a

dual purpose – they can be served for afternoon

tea as well. Fritters are traditionally served at

Christmas and at carnival time. The reason for this

is probably that at those times the ovens were

so taken up with the cooking of meats, breads and

large cakes that certain of the sweet dishes

had to be fried instead of baked.

To round off a meal, home-made sweets are often

served with a mature Port wine or an old Madeira.

# Fritters

# Portuguese Dreams
## *Sonhos Portugueses*

The name derives from the fact that these fritters are feather-light and almost hollow inside.

| | |
|---|---|
| 200 ml water | *Syrup* |
| pinch of salt | 250 g sugar |
| strip of lemon rind | 150 ml water |
| 20 g sugar | strip of lemon rind |
| 25 g butter | strip of orange rind |
| 100 g flour | 1 stick cinnamon |
| 25 g cornflour (maizena) | 50 ml Port wine |
| 3 eggs | |
| oil for frying | |

**To make the fritters:** Place the water, salt, lemon rind, sugar and butter in a saucepan. Bring to the boil. Add the sifted flour and maizena. Mix well until a ball is formed. Cool. Add the eggs one at a time, beating well after each addition. Fry spoonfuls of the batter in deep oil, 2 – 3 at a time, until golden brown. Drain on paper towelling. Dip into a mixture of sugar and ground cinnamon, or make the syrup and pour it over the 'dreams'.

**To make the syrup:** Boil the sugar, water, rinds and cinnamon for 15 minutes. Remove the rinds. Add the Port wine and pour over the 'dreams'.

# Dough Rings
## *Filhós*

| | |
|---|---|
| 500 g bread dough (see p150) | 5 ml baking powder |
| 3 eggs | 250 ml cooked pumpkin |
| 125 ml orange juice | 250 ml flour (approximately) |
| 25 ml brandy *(aguardente)* | cooking oil for frying |

Place all the ingredients, except the flour, in a bowl. (A food mixer may also be used.) Beat well, adding the extra flour a little at a time until a soft but not sticky dough is obtained – bubbles should appear on the surface. Cover the mixture and let it rise until it has doubled in size.

Dip your hands in water. Take pieces of dough, shape them into rings and fry them in hot oil. Drain and sprinkle with cinnamon sugar.

# Tipsy Slices
## *Rabanadas*

These are traditionally served on Christmas Eve.

| | |
|---|---|
| 1 French loaf (day-old bread | *Syrup* |
|   is best) | 500 g sugar |
| 2 eggs | 250 ml water |
| 125 ml milk | 1 stick cinnamon |
| 5 ml grated lemon rind | 50 ml Port wine |
| oil for frying | |

Cut the bread into slices about 2 cm thick. Beat the eggs and place in a soup plate. Mix the milk and lemon rind and pour into a separate soup plate. Dip the bread slices into the milk and then into the beaten egg. Fry in hot oil. Drain well.

To make the syrup, boil the sugar and water for 3 minutes. Dip each fried bread slice into the hot syrup and then place in a deep serving bowl. Add the cinnamon stick and Port wine to the remaining syrup, bring to the boil and pour over the slices of fried bread.

**Variation**
*Fatias:* Sprinkle the bread with cinnamon and sugar after frying.

# Carnival Fritters
## *Malassadas*

These are usually made on Shrove Tuesday. They were traditionally made from yeast dough, but nowadays the busy housewife has to use quicker methods. Be cautious when you receive a gift of *malassadas*, especially during carnival time, as strange fillings are sometimes used to play a trick on one!

| | |
|---|---|
| 250 ml water | 30 ml sugar |
| 5 ml aniseed | 4 eggs |
| strip of lemon rind | oil for frying |
| 1 stick cinnamon | |
| 500 ml flour | *Syrup* |
| 7 ml baking powder | 375 ml water |
| pinch of salt | 250 ml sugar |

Boil the water, aniseed, lemon rind and cinnamon for 5 minutes. Strain and cool slightly.

Sift the flour, baking powder and salt into a bowl. Add the sugar. Make a well in the centre and beat in the eggs and enough of the flavoured water to make a soft batter. Fry spoonfuls of the batter in hot oil, drain and 'drown' in the syrup or in honey.

To make the syrup, dissolve the sugar in the water and boil for 5 minutes.


# Pumpkin Stems
## *Farturas (Churros, Pés de Abóbora)*

These are sold at fêtes, markets, fairs and bazaars. A large syringe is usually used for making them but I find that a pastry bag fitted with a large fluted nozzle is equally successful.

| | |
|---|---|
| 1 litre water | 500 g flour |
| 20 ml sugar | 20 ml Port wine |
| 20 g butter | 3 – 4 eggs |
| pinch of salt | oil for frying |
| 1 stick cinnamon | cinnamon sugar |
| strip of lemon rind | |

Place the water, sugar, butter, salt, cinnamon and lemon rind in a saucepan. Bring to the boil and then add the sifted flour, mixing it in very quickly. Cook for 1 – 2 minutes. Remove from the heat and cool. Add the Port wine. Mix in the eggs one at a time, beating well until the mixture is of a soft consistency.

Heat the cooking oil in a saucepan. Place the mixture in a piping bag fitted with a nozzle. Starting in the centre of the saucepan, pipe the dough in a spiral shape. Fry until golden on both sides – be very careful when you turn it over. Remove from the oil and drain on kitchen paper. Cut into pieces with a pair of scissors and sprinkle with cinnamon sugar.

**Variation**
Pipe and fry long strips of dough. These are called 'pumpkin stems' (*pés de abóbora*).

# Nógados

Another of my childhood favourites. I remember my mother and her friends making these delicacies and serving them on orange leaves. Traditionally the dough was cooked in hot honey and only olive oil was used. These are made at carnival time (not used as tricks but certainly tricky to make) in the Alentejo province.

| | |
|---|---|
| 10 ml brandy | 30 ml grated orange rind |
| 3 eggs | pinch of salt |
| 15 ml olive oil | 250 ml flour (approximately) |
| 10 ml cooking oil | 300 ml honey |
| 15 ml castor sugar | |

Beat the brandy, eggs, oils, castor sugar, orange rind and salt until fluffy. Add enough sifted flour to make a soft pliable dough (similar to pastry dough). Cut off small pieces of dough and roll them into sticks about 5 – 6 mm thick. Cut into pieces 1 cm long and keep apart on a kitchen cloth covered with flour.

Bring the honey to the boil and carefully add the little cubes of dough. Stir with a slotted spoon and remove when golden brown. Place on a greased tray to dry.

If orange leaves are available, place a tablespoon of fried cubes on each washed leaf. Otherwise, serve in paper cases.

**Variations**
* If you are feeling adventurous, scoop the cooked cubes of dough on to an oiled surface and roll, while hot, into a sausage shape. Cool and then cut into slices.
* Fry the small cubes in hot cooking oil for 2 – 3 minutes. Drain the cubes, add them to hot honey, bring to the boil and then remove.

# Vitoria's Rings
## *Argolinhas da Dona Vitória*

3 eggs
75 ml olive oil (*or* half olive
    oil, half cooking oil)
750 ml flour
15 ml baking powder
125 ml warm water
oil for frying

*Syrup*
250 ml water
500 ml sugar

Beat the eggs with the oil until pale. Add the flour, baking powder and enough warm water to make a dough. Grease your hands with olive oil and knead the dough well. Allow to rest for at least 20 minutes. Grease hands with olive oil again and break off pieces of dough the size of a walnut. Roll with the palms of the hands into a strip and close the ends of the strip together to form a ring. Score around the surface of the ring with a knife. Deep-fry the rings in oil and drain.

In a large pot, dissolve the sugar in the water, bring to the boil and boil for 5 minutes. Place all the rings in the syrup and place the pot over a low heat for 5 minutes. Remove from the heat and toss the pan carefully to avoid breaking the rings, but making sure that they all have a thick coating of the syrup.

# Sweet Potato Puffs
## *Azevias, Empanadilhas*

*Pastry*
250 g flour
pinch of salt
25 ml olive oil
20 g butter
50 ml brandy
25 ml cooking oil
25 ml orange juice
3 eggs
5 ml ground cinnamon
oil for frying

*Filling*
250 g sugar
100 ml water
250 g cooked and mashed
    sweet potato
125 ml grated orange rind
2 ml ground cinnamon
125 ml nibbed almonds

*To make the pastry:* Sift the flour and the salt. Mix the oil and butter together and warm over a low heat. Pour the hot oil and butter over the flour and mix. Mix in the rest of the ingredients and add enough warm water to make a soft dough. Knead well and then rest the dough for 1 hour.

*To make the filling:* Boil the sugar and water for 5 minutes. Mix in the sweet potato and the orange rind and boil until thick. Add the cinnamon and almonds and allow to cool.

Grease a pastry board (better still, a marble slab) and rolling pin with oil. Roll out the pastry *very* thinly. Place teaspoonfuls of the filling a few centimetres apart on one half of the pastry. Fold over the other half of the pastry and, using a pastry wheel, cut into squares around the spoonfuls of filling – they will resemble little cushions. Fry in medium-hot oil until puffed-up and golden, drain and sprinkle with cinnamon and sugar.

### Variation

As an alternative filling, combine 500 g cooked chick peas, 350 g sugar, 10 ml grated lemon rind and 1 egg yolk. Proceed as above.

# Pastry Swirls
## *Filhós Enroladas*

My Aunt Pétinha has finally succeeded in teaching me the art of making these pastries. All you need is a little patience and a touch of dexterity, and these will be the talk of the party.

Make the pastry as described in the recipe for Sweet Potato Puffs. Roll it out very thinly and cut into strips 30 cm by 5 cm. Hold one end of a strip with your left hand and with your right hand anchor the other end with a fork. Then lower the 'forked' end of the pastry strip into hot oil and turn the fork repeatedly until all the pastry has been rolled into a spiral. Remove the fork and continue frying the pastry 'rosette' until it is golden brown. Remove from the oil and drain. Sprinkle with cinnamon sugar.

# Desserts
## *Sobremesas*

The recipes that follow are for formal desserts, usually served only on special occasions.

# Portuguese Crème Caramel
## *Pudim de Copo*

From a culinary point of view this recipe is not the correct way to make a crème caramel, but it is a very easy and flop-proof method of preparing this traditional pudding.

Sometimes called the '365 Pudding' because it is served every day of the year, every Portuguese housewife has one or more special tins in which to cook it and probably also a thousand variations of the recipe. If you are baking the pudding in the oven use an ordinary cake tin. If you are cooking it in a pressure cooker use an ovenproof glass bowl and cover the top with a double layer of tin foil.

| | |
|---|---|
| 250 ml sugar for the caramel | 1 glass of milk |
| 1 glass of eggs (use a tumbler) | 10 ml grated lemon rind |
| 1 glass of sugar | 25 ml Port wine |

First make the caramel by placing the 250 ml sugar in a heavy saucepan and melting over a low heat until it turns golden. Line a pudding tin or bowl with the caramel.

In a bowl beat the eggs, sugar, milk, lemon rind and Port wine. Do not overbeat. Strain this mixture into the caramel-lined tin or bowl. Place in a bain-marie containing sufficient hot water to reach half-way up the side of the tin or bowl. Bake in the oven at 140° C for about an hour, or until firm, or cook in a pressure cooker for 5 minutes. Leave it inside the pressure cooker until it is cool. Place in the refrigerator overnight. Invert on to a platter just before serving.

**Variation**
Substitute orange juice or crushed pineapple for the milk and add any orange liqueur instead of the Port.

# Coffee Crème Caramel
## *Pudim de Café*

250 ml sugar for the caramel
6 eggs
397 ml sweetened condensed milk

375 ml cold coffee
125 ml cream
25 ml Port wine or coffee
liqueur

Make the caramel by placing the sugar in a heavy saucepan and melting over a low heat until it turns golden. Line a pudding tin or bowl with the caramel.

Beat the eggs. Add the condensed milk, cold coffee, cream and Port wine or coffee liqueur, and stir lightly. Pour the mixture into the caramel-lined tin or bowl. Place in a bain-marie containing enough hot water to reach half-way up the side of the tin or bowl. Bake at 140° C for about an hour. Refrigerate overnight and invert on to a platter just before serving.

# Papaw Pudding
## *Pudim de Papaia*

This traditional Madeiran pudding is for the daring cook.

1 kg papaw
4 eggs
500 ml milk
300 g sugar

5 ml grated lemon rind
5 ml grated orange rind
50 g butter
50 g flour or cornflour

Peel and seed the papaw. Cook it in a little water until it is tender. Place in a colander and drain well – preferably overnight. Mash to a fine pulp. Add the remaining ingredients, beat well and pour into a caramelised pudding tin (see recipe for Crème Caramel, p134). Pressure-cook or bake as for Crème Caramel.

Two more recipes for the daring cook . . . If you are not very keen on bacon-and-beans, how about separating them? Use bacon in the following recipe and beans in the one after that . . .

## *Pudim do Abade de Priscos*

This recipe originated in the town of Priscos. In his spare time the parish priest *(Abade)* of Priscos indulged in such hobbies as fine embroidery and cookery, although he was very secretive about his culinary successes. He is alleged to have said that the art of cooking depended entirely on the artist. Unfortunately he did not leave any written records of his recipes and only a few people remember some of them.

This is a most unusual combination of fatty bacon, eggs and sugar, but it is worth trying.

| | |
|---|---|
| 500 ml water | strip of lemon rind |
| 500 g sugar | 1 stick cinnamon |
| 40 g rindless bacon fat | 50 ml Port wine |
| (use smoked bacon) | 14 egg yolks |

Place the water, sugar, fat, lemon rind and cinnamon stick in a saucepan. Dissolve the sugar over a low heat and then bring to the boil and simmer for 5 – 6 minutes. Strain the liquid and allow it to cool. Add the wine and the beaten egg yolks. Mix well, but do not beat. Pour into a caramelised tin (see p134) and bake in a bain-marie at 180° C for 1 hour, or until set.

## Haricot Pudding
### *Pudim de Feijão*

| | |
|---|---|
| 500 g sugar | 8 egg yolks |
| 250 ml water | 6 whole eggs |
| 250 ml dried haricot beans | 250 ml orange juice |
| (soaked, cooked and mashed | 10 ml grated orange rind |
| to a fine purée) | |

Place the sugar and water in a saucepan and boil for 3 minutes exactly. Add the bean purée. Mix well and then cool completely. Add the beaten egg yolks, the beaten eggs, orange juice and orange rind. Mix well. Pour into a caramelised tin (see p134) and bake in a bain-marie at 180° C for 1 hour, or until set.

# Rice Pudding
## *Arroz Doce*

A party is not a party without *Arroz Doce*. Served in individual portions or on a large platter, it is always available as a dessert in Portuguese restaurants.

| | |
|---|---|
| 125 g rice | 200 g sugar |
| 250 ml water | 25 g butter |
| pinch of salt | 3 egg yolks |
| 500 ml milk, warmed | 10 ml grated lemon rind |
| 1 stick cinnamon | ground cinnamon for |
| strip of lemon rind | decoration |

Boil the rice in salted water for 10 minutes. Strain. Add the warm milk, cinnamon stick and lemon rind. Simmer until the rice is cooked. Remove the cinnamon stick and the lemon rind. Add the sugar and butter and continue cooking for 5 – 10 minutes.

Beat the egg yolks. Add a little of the warm rice mixture to the egg yolks, mix well and pour into the saucepan. Simmer for 2 – 3 minutes, stirring continuously. Add the grated lemon rind.

Pour into individual serving bowls or on to a large platter (do not forget to leave a little in the saucepan for the cook). Sprinkle with ground cinnamon or decorate Portuguese-style. The easiest way to do this is to dip a fancy pastry or biscuit cutter into cinnamon and make patterns on the surface of the rice. When rice pudding was served at weddings it was customary to decorate it with the initials of the bride and groom.

# Rich Pasta Pudding
## *Aletria*

We have a recipe for pasta after all – even if it is for a sweet dish. The pasta used in Portugal is a very thin vermicelli sometimes called *Cabelo de Anjo* ('angels' hair'). In the original recipe for this pudding a syrup was made of sugar and water and the precooked vermicelli and egg yolks were added afterwards. As with everything else, recipes have also changed . . .

| | |
|---|---|
| 100 g vermicelli | 1 stick cinnamon |
| 500 ml milk | 45 ml butter |
| 125 g castor sugar | 4 egg yolks |
| strip of lemon rind | ground cinnamon |

Boil the vermicelli in 750 ml water for 5 minutes. Drain. Add the milk, sugar, lemon rind and cinnamon stick to the vermicelli. Bring to the boil and simmer until soft. Add the butter and the beaten egg yolks. Simmer just long enough to cook the egg yolks. Pour into a large serving dish, dust with cinnamon and serve.

This pudding is best eaten on the day that it is made.

## Pudim Molotov

No one seems to be sure of the origin of this pudding. It is a delicious baked combination of egg whites and caramel topped, of course, with *Ovos Moles* (see p185). The only explanation for the name that I can think of is that someone had an explosion in the oven the first time he or she made it.

The making of this pudding is a delicate matter. When I was first given the recipe I was told to wait until the chickens had laid fresh eggs, to close all doors (no draughts allowed), and to disconnect the telephone.

| | |
|---|---|
| 200 g sugar for the caramel | 200 g sugar |
| 12 egg whites | 125 ml toasted nuts for |
| 3 ml cream of tartar | garnishing |

*Sauce: Ovos Moles* made from the 12 egg yolks (see p185)

Preheat the oven to 200° C. Place a deep baking tray half-filled with cold water in the oven. Grease a large ring tin. Make the caramel by melting the 200 g sugar over a low heat until it is golden. Beat the egg whites with the cream of tartar until stiff. Gradually beat in the sugar. Pour the caramel in a stream into the egg whites, beating all the time. Pour into the greased tin and place in the tray of water in the oven. After 10 minutes, lower the temperature to 180° C and bake for a further 5 minutes. Switch the oven off and leave the pudding in the oven for 15 – 20 minutes. Open the oven door slightly and leave the pudding in the oven until cold.

Remove from the tin and pour the sauce over the pudding. Sprinkle with toasted nuts.

Good luck!

# Bolo Pudim

This is a recipe to satisfy all tastes: if you want pudding for dessert, you eat the top; if you want cake, you eat the bottom. If you are like me, you eat both.

250 ml sugar for the caramel
butter

**Pudding**
4 eggs
250 ml sugar
10 ml grated lemon rind
300 ml milk

*Cake*
4 eggs, separated
60 ml sugar
5 ml vanilla essence
60 ml flour
5 ml baking powder

Make the caramel (see p134) and line a large ring tin with it. Allow to cool. When cold, grease with butter.

*To prepare the pudding:* Beat the eggs with the sugar and lemon rind, mix in the milk and pour into the prepared pan.

*To prepare the cake:* Beat the egg yolks, sugar and vanilla essence. Add the flour and baking powder and fold in the stiffly beaten egg whites. Spoon this mixture *very carefully* over the pudding.

Bake in an oven preheated to 180° C for 40 – 50 minutes. Before turning it out test with a skewer or toothpick to make sure that it is cooked. Loosen the edges with a knife and turn out into a deep plate.

Enjoy it!

# Milk Pudding
## *Sericaia, Cerica*

This is our version of milk tart. It is believed that this recipe was brought to Portugal from India. It was served at royal banquets on beautiful pewter plates.

| | |
|---|---|
| 6 eggs, separated | 500 ml milk |
| 250 g sugar | 1 stick cinnamon |
| 10 ml grated lemon rind | ground cinnamon |
| 100 ml flour | |

Beat the egg yolks with the sugar and lemon rind until creamy. Blend the flour with the milk and stir into the yolk mixture. Add the cinnamon stick. Pour into a saucepan, bring to the boil and cook until thick, stirring all the time. Remove from the heat and allow to cool slightly. Remove the cinnamon stick and fold in the stiffly beaten egg whites.

Spoon into a greased ovenproof dish. Alternate the spoonfuls – one horizontal, one vertical – and sprinkle ground cinnamon between each spoonful.

Bake in a very hot oven (200° C) for 15 – 20 minutes, or until it is well-risen and split across the top.

**The two recipes that follow have been lovingly adopted. Don't try to tell anyone that they are not traditionally Portuguese – unless you want to start an argument.**

# Clouds
## *Nuvens ou Farofias*

| | |
|---|---|
| 4 eggs, separated | 25 ml sugar |
| pinch of cream of tartar | 1 vanilla pod |
| 100 g sugar | 25 ml sugar |
| 500 ml milk | 10 ml cornflour |

Beat the egg whites and cream of tartar until they form soft peaks. Gradually add 100 g sugar and beat until the mixture forms stiff peaks.

Heat the milk, 25 ml sugar and the vanilla pod until just simmering. Remove the vanilla pod. Poach spoonfuls of the egg white mixture in the milk

*Clockwise from the left*
Sponge Cake; Orange Roll; Assorted Tartlets; Assorted Biscuits

*Clockwise from the left*
Pastry Swirls; Stuffed Turkey; King's Crown Cake;
Christmas Eve Cod; Dough Rings;
Madeiran 'Honey' Cake; Tipsy Slices

for about 2 minutes on each side. Remove with a slotted spoon and allow to drain on paper towel. Continue until all the egg whites have been used.

Make a custard using the remaining milk (add more if necessary to make up to 500 ml and taste for sweetness). Beat the egg yolks with 25 ml sugar until smooth. Add the cornflour. Pour the hot milk over this mixture and stir well. Return the mixture to the saucepan and cook over a gentle heat until it thickens, stirring all the time. Do not allow the mixture to boil.

Pour the custard into a deep glass plate and arrange the egg-white 'clouds' on top. Dust with ground cinnamon or drizzle with caramel. For 'dark clouds' place under the grill for a few seconds.

# Chocolate Mousse
## *Mousse de Chocolate*

6 eggs, separated
100 g castor sugar
5 ml grated orange rind
300 g dark chocolate
15 ml butter

6 ml instant coffee
   powder/granules
2 ml ground cinnamon
250 ml cream, whipped
pinch of salt
100 g castor sugar

Separate the eggs. Beat the egg yolks, 100 g castor sugar and orange rind until pale. Melt the chocolate in a double-boiler. Add the butter, coffee and cinnamon. Add the chocolate mixture to the egg yolk mixture and mix well. Fold in the whipped cream.

Beat the egg whites with a pinch of salt until stiff, adding 100 g castor sugar gradually. Fold into the chocolate mixture. Pour into a glass bowl and refrigerate overnight.

# Egg Custard
## *Leite Creme*

This is the simplest of puddings, characterised by the 'burnt' flavour acquired by burning the top of the pudding with a special iron. The burning irons are made from an iron rod with a wooden handle. At the end of the rod a flat iron shape is attached – it may be shaped like a heart or a flower, or may be a simple circle. The iron is heated until red-hot and the shapes are burnt on to the top of the custard.

| | |
|---|---|
| 500 ml milk | 10 ml grated lemon rind |
| 6 egg yolks | 15 ml flour |
| 125 g sugar | |

Heat the milk. Beat the egg yolks with the sugar and lemon rind until fluffy. Dissolve the flour in a little cold milk. Add it to the egg mixture and stir well. Add the warm milk. Pour the mixture into a saucepan. Bring to boiling point and cook for 2 – 3 minutes until thick, stirring all the time. Do not allow the mixture to boil.

Pour into an ovenproof dish and sprinkle with a little sugar.

Unless you are married to an ironmonger who can make you a rod very quickly, I suggest you place the pudding under the grill to 'burn'.

# Golden Soup
## *Sopa Dourada*

There must be something exquisite about this dish to have earned it a mention in a book by one of our most famous authors, Eça de Queirós. It is traditionally served at Christmas-time in the north of Portugal. This recipe is another example of the art of *aproveitar* (use of left-overs).

| | |
|---|---|
| 400 g sugar | 8 egg yolks |
| 200 ml water | toasted almonds or pine |
| strip of naartjie rind | kernels to garnish |
| 250 g day-old sponge cake, | |
|    cut into slices | |

Place the sugar, water and naartjie rind in a saucepan over a low heat. When the sugar has dissolved bring the mixture to the boil. Boil for 5 minutes and then remove from the heat. Dip the cake slices very quickly into the syrup and place them in an overlapping arrangement in a glass serving dish. Beat the egg yolks. Add a little of the hot syrup to them and then pour them into the saucepan containing the rest of the syrup. Return to the heat and simmer until thick. Pour over the slices of cake and sprinkle with toasted almonds or pine kernels.

**Variation**
Add toasted almonds and 15 ml butter to the syrup. Add the beaten egg yolks and the sponge cake cut into cubes. Mix well. Pour into a glass bowl and sprinkle with cinnamon.

# Chestnut Pudding
## *Pudim de Chocolate e Castanhas*

Because we have our Christmas in summer in South Africa, I often serve this pudding instead of some of the more usual baked delicacies.

| | |
|---|---|
| 200 g butter | 10 ml grated orange rind |
| 200 g icing sugar | 200 ml orange juice |
| 250 g cooking chocolate, melted | 1 tin (500 g) chestnut purée |
| 50 ml orange liqueur | |

Beat the butter and icing sugar until creamy. Add the melted chocolate. Fold in all the remaining ingredients. Pour into a lined loaf tin or a greased ring mould. Refrigerate until set. Unmould and decorate with cherries and holly leaves.

This pudding freezes well.

# Sweets
## *Doces*

To round off a meal, serve these home-made sweets with a mature Port wine or an old Madeira. They also make ideal gifts. The ingredients are so similar that one could make a large batch of egg and syrup mixture and cut and shape into the different sweets.

Almonds are an important ingredient in Portuguese sweets, particularly the hand-made confectionery from the Algarve. Visitors to the Algarve in early spring are dazzled by the magnificence of the almond blossoms which spread in broad bands of white across fields and hillsides, giving the impression of freshly-fallen snow. There is a charming legend about the origin of the Algarve's almond trees . . . Many centuries ago a Moorish king married a princess from a cold northern land. Observing that his bride was filled with nostalgia for the snow-covered meadows of her homeland, the king ordered the planting of the almond trees so that, once a year, she could view a landscape that would remind her of her childhood home . . .

# Carrot and Orange Sweets
## *Laranjinhas da China*

Oranges were originally imported from China. The Portuguese started growing them during the seventeenth century.

| | |
|---|---|
| 1 bunch carrots | castor sugar |
| sugar | cloves |
| 25 ml grated orange rind | |

Peel and slice the carrots and boil until tender. Drain and then blend until smooth. Weigh the carrots. Place in a saucepan and add the same weight in sugar. Add the orange rind. Cook over a low heat, stirring all the time, until thick and almost dry. Cool. Shape into small balls and roll in castor sugar. Place each ball in a small paper cup. Stick a clove in the centre and attach a small orange leaf (or a small leaf cut out of angelica).

# Sweet Chestnuts
## *Castanhas de Ovos*

125 g sugar
50 ml water
8 egg yolks

Boil the sugar and water. Cool slightly and add the beaten egg yolks. Cook over a low heat, stirring all the time, until the bottom of the saucepan is visible when stirring. Place on a greased board and leave until cold.

Dust a working surface with sugar and roll the mixture to form a long sausage. Cut into small pieces the size of chestnuts. Shape into chestnuts, flattening each one slightly with a fork. Brush with beaten egg yolk. Holding each sweet on a fondue fork, scorch over a flame so that they resemble roasted chestnuts. Serve in paper cases.

**Variation**
*Nozes de Cascais:* Prepare the mixture as above. (Ground almonds are sometimes added.) Shape into round balls. Place half a walnut in the centre of each ball and press in lightly. Make a caramel with 70 g sugar and 25 ml water. Working very quickly and using two forks, dip each ball into the caramel and place on a greased surface. Place in paper cups when cool.

# Mother-in-law's Eyes
## *Olhos de Sogra*

As I am a mother-in-law myself, I have no comments about this recipe.

| | |
|---|---|
| 350 g sugar | coating chocolate |
| 400 g ground almonds | silver dragees |
| 3 egg yolks | |

Place the sugar and almonds in a saucepan with a little water. Bring to the boil and simmer until dry. Add the beaten egg yolks. Cook for a further 2 minutes and then cool. Shape into round sweets. With your finger make an indentation in the centre of each sweet and fill with melted chocolate. Place a silver dragee in the middle of the chocolate.

**Variation**
Cut prunes in half and remove the stone. Fill with the almond mixture. Roll in sugar and place a currant in the middle of the almond mixture.

# Egg Sweets
## *Rebuçados de Ovos*
## *(Gemas de Ovos)*

These were very popular when I was a child. I remember cutting fringes on the colourful squares of paper that were used to wrap these delicious sweets.

| | |
|---|---|
| 250 g sugar | 8 egg yolks |
| 125 ml water | 300 g sugar for coating |
| 250 g ground almonds | a few drops of lemon juice |

Place the sugar and water in a saucepan over a low heat. When the sugar has dissolved, boil the mixture for 2 minutes. Remove from the heat and add the almonds and lightly beaten egg yolks. Return to the heat and continue cooking, stirring all the time, until you can see the bottom of the pan. Allow to cool. Lightly grease your hands and roll pieces of the mixture into small round balls. Place on a greased surface (a marble slab is ideal).

For the coating, boil the sugar in a little water until it begins to 'thread'. (Take a teaspoon of the syrup and tip it out over a dish. If the syrup forms a fine thin thread as it drops into the dish, it has reached the 'thread' stage.)

Remove from the heat. Beat the sugar until it is opaque, adding a few drops of lemon juice. Keep the sugar mixture warm in a bain-marie. Using two forks and working very quickly, dip each almond sweet into the coating and place on a greased surface. When cold, wrap in colourful paper or place in small paper cases.

# Figs Stuffed With Almonds
## *Figos Cheios*

| | |
|---|---|
| 100 g nibbed almonds | 15 ml drinking chocolate |
| 5 ml ground cinnamon | powder |
| 2 ml ground aniseed | 250 g sugar |
| | dried figs |

Mix the almonds, ground cinnamon, ground aniseed, drinking chocolate and sugar in a bowl. Slit the figs lengthwise and stretch them. Fill with the almond mixture. Press the figs closed. Place them on a baking tray and roast in a medium oven (150° C) until they are brown. When cool wrap in fringed paper. These figs are sometimes plaited together into strings – they look rather like garlic strings.

**Variation**
Cut the figs in half across their width. Place a whole almond in one half of each fig, and close with the other half. Press together and roast as above. Sometimes the figs are cut into star shapes and filled and roasted as described above.

# Fig and Almond Sweets
## *Doce de Figo*

The making of these sweets is an art practised nowhere else in the world but the Algarve. The paste is traditionally moulded into animal shapes – hens, rabbits, fishes, dogs, cats, etc. I usually just roll the paste into little balls so that I don't feel sorry when I eat them.

| | |
|---|---|
| 250 g whole blanched almonds | 250 g sugar |
| *or* 250 g nibbed almonds | 100 ml water |
| 250 g dried figs | 30 g drinking chocolate |
| | powder |

Soften the almonds and figs in a cool oven (100° C) for 30 minutes. Place separately in a blender and chop roughly. Place the sugar and water in a saucepan over a low heat. When the sugar has dissolved bring to the boil and boil for 2 – 3 minutes. Add the almonds, figs and drinking chocolate powder and continue cooking, stirring constantly, until you can see the bottom of the pan. Cool slightly. While the paste is still warm, roll into balls or shape as wished. Coat with sugar and wrap in fringed paper.

# Almond Sweets
## *Doces de Amêndoa*

There cannot be anything more delicious or more pleasing to the eye than these sweets. All you need is a little patience and an artistic touch. Consult cake-decorating books for ideas. The paste is usually shaped into fruits, baskets, vegetables, hams, etc. which are painted with food colourings so that they resemble the real thing. They are usually about 3 – 5 cm in size. Ready-made marzipan may be used, but the taste is not the same.

| | |
|---|---|
| 250 g ground almonds | food colourings |
| 250 g icing sugar | *Ovos Moles* (see p185) |
| 1 egg white | *Fios de Ovos* (see p183) |

Mix the almonds and icing sugar with enough lightly beaten egg white to form a marzipan paste. Colour the marzipan with food colouring, according to what you are planning to shape it into – eg orange for carrots, green for leaves. Use a small amount of *Ovos Moles* as a filling for each 'sculpture' and *Fios de Ovos* for decorating.

# Breads and Cakes
## *Pão e Bolos*

In rural areas it is still customary for people to bake

their own bread in clay ovens once a week.

Neighbours organise a sort of roster so that

each one bakes on a different day.

I have adapted the bread recipes so that they are

suitable for an electric oven. A mixture of flours

(eg cake flour, bread flour and wholewheat flour)

will produce a result that is closest to genuine

Portuguese bread. The best time to make bread is

after you have had a row with someone, or when

you would like to have an argument with someone

who is not there . . . try knocking some dough

around. It is better than counting to ten!

The Portuguese love of yeast cookery is reflected

not only in bread-making but in dozens of

dough-based cakes.

# Breads
## *Pão*

# Home-made Bread
## *Pão Cazeiro*

25 g yeast (1 cake)
5 ml sugar
125 ml warm water
1 kg cake flour
500 g bread flour

250 ml wholewheat flour
10 ml salt
250 ml grated raw potato *or*
    250 ml cooked sweet potato
750 ml warm water
    (approximately)

Mix the yeast and the sugar with 125 ml warm water. Sprinkle with a little flour and leave for 10 – 15 minutes to form a sponge. Sift the flours. Add the salt, potato and yeast mixture and knead, adding the warm water gradually. Knead until small bubbles appear in the dough. Sprinkle a little flour over the dough and cover with a tablecloth and a small rug. (Most Portuguese households keep a large basin and a cloth and blanket just for making bread.)

Let the dough rise until double in size (45 minutes – 1 hour, depending on the weather). Punch down well and shape into round loaves. Place a tablecloth on the kitchen table and place each loaf, slightly apart, on the cloth. Dust with flour. Cover and again allow to rise until double in size.

Meanwhile, place some baking sheets in an oven preheated to 200° C. Dust the sheets with flour just before placing the bread in the oven. Place the loaves on the hot baking sheets and bake for 30 minutes. Lower the temperature to 180° C and continue baking until cooked. Bread is done when it sounds hollow when tapped on the top and the bottom.

Bread is shaped in different ways in different parts of Portugal. Some loaves are round and others are scored across the top. I prefer to hold the loaf around the middle and flip one half over the other.

**Makes 4 loaves.**

# Portuguese Rolls
## *Papo-secos*

Follow the above recipe, using 1 kg cake flour only. If a smaller quantity is required, halve the ingredients.

After the dough has risen the first time, form into oval shapes with a point at either end. Roll the points slightly. Score the surface, dust with lots of flour and leave to rise for a second time. Bake in a hot oven (190° C) for 20 – 25 minutes, or until cooked.

# Stone Bread
## *Bolo de (do) Caco*

This bread is typical of Madeira. It should be baked in an earthenware frying pan – hence the name *caco*. It so happens that my father's name is Caco. When he first met my future in-laws, he thought he was being honoured by having special bread baked for him on that day. He was a little disappointed to discover that the people of Madeira had been baking this bread for centuries before he was born.

The bread should be eaten on the day it is made (it is best the moment it comes out of the 'oven') with lots of butter, or it can be frozen. The following recipe is my adaptation, using an electric frying pan. (Why use a *caco* when I already have it for a name?)

| | |
|---|---|
| 1 kg cake flour | 5 ml sugar |
| 25 ml salt | 250 g cooked and mashed |
| 25 g yeast (1 cake) | sweet potato |
| | 1 litre warm water |

Sift the flour and salt into the bowl of a food mixer equipped with a dough hook. Mix the yeast with the sugar and 125 ml warm water. Leave for 5 minutes, then add to the flour with the sweet potato. Slowly add enough warm water to form a dough. Mix for 5 – 6 minutes until the dough comes away from the sides of the bowl. Cover and allow to rise for 30 – 40 minutes.

Place the dough on a floured board and divide into about 8 round cakes. Flatten until 2 cm thick. Cover. Meanwhile warm an electric frying pan on high and dust with flour. Place the bread in the hot pan. Turn the bread when a crust has formed and bake the other side. Carefully hold the bread upright and bake the sides, turning as it cooks. When done place on a kitchen cloth and cover to retain a soft texture.

# Mealie Meal Bread
## *Broa de Milho*

10 ml salt
500 ml hot water
500 g mealie meal
25 g yeast (1 cake)
5 ml sugar

125 ml warm water
500 g cake flour
500 g bread flour
500 ml lukewarm water

Dissolve the salt in 500 ml hot water and pour over the mealie meal. Mix and leave to cool. Mix the yeast with the sugar and 125 ml warm water. Leave for 5 minutes. Add the yeast mixture and the remaining ingredients to the mealie meal and knead well. Shape into round loaves, place on a floured tablecloth and allow to rise until double in size. Bake on flour-dusted baking sheets in a very hot oven (200° C) for 15 minutes. Reduce the temperature to 180° C and continue baking until the bread sounds hollow when tapped on top and bottom.

# Cocktail Rolls
## *Pãezinhos de Leite*

It is a Portuguese custom to have a mid-afternoon snack called *lanche*. Children usually have a glass of milk, juice or chocolate and a *pãozinho* filled with either cheese or ham.

25 g yeast (1 cake)
60 ml warm water
60 ml sugar
60 g butter

300 ml buttermilk, warmed
1 egg
5 ml salt
400 g flour

Dissolve the yeast in the warm water with 5 ml sugar. Leave for 5 minutes. Melt the butter in the buttermilk. Place the milk mixture in the bowl of an electric mixer and combine it with the yeast mixture, the sugar, egg, salt and 150 g flour. Beat on low speed for 1 minute and then on medium speed for 2 minutes. Add the rest of the flour and continue beating until a soft (but not sticky) dough is formed. Beat for a further 5 minutes. Cover and allow to rise for 30 minutes. Knock down. Break off 50 g portions and roll into balls or oval shapes. Cover and again allow to rise until double in size. Brush with a mixture of beaten egg and water. Bake at 200° C for 15 – 20 minutes.

# Chouriço Rolls
## Pãezinhos de Chouriço

Use either the bread roll (p151) or the cocktail roll (p152) recipe. After the dough has risen for the first time, take a piece of dough the size of a tennis ball, flatten it and place slices of *chouriço* or a whole piece of *chouriço* in the centre. Fold the sides of the dough towards the middle and roll. Prick with a fork, or score the surface slightly, to allow steam to escape. Cover, and allow to rise until double in size. Dust with flour and bake at 200° C for 20 – 25 minutes.

# God's Bread
## Pão de Deus

This bread is traditionally served on All Saints' Day, although many bakeries sell it all year round.

| | |
|---|---|
| 25 g yeast (1 cake) | *Paste* |
| 5 ml sugar | 2 egg whites |
| 500 g flour | 5 ml grated lemon rind |
| 3 eggs | 100 g desiccated coconut |
| 150 g butter | 75 ml sugar |
| 200 g sugar | 1 egg yolk, beaten |
| 10 ml grated orange rind | icing sugar for dredging |
| 10 ml grated lemon rind | |
| 400 ml milk | |
| 250 g mixed glacé fruits, chopped | |
| 100 ml orange juice | |

Mix the yeast with 5 ml sugar and 125 ml warm water. Leave for 5 minutes. Sift the flour into a bowl and make a well in the centre. Add the yeast mixture, lightly beaten eggs, butter, sugar, grated rinds and warm milk. Knead well, adding more flour if necessary. Cover and allow to rise until double in size. Add the fruits which have previously been soaked in the orange juice. Knead well and then shape into small round cakes. Place on floured baking sheets and allow to rise once more.

Meanwhile make the paste by mixing together the lightly beaten egg whites, the grated lemon rind, coconut and sugar. Brush the cakes with beaten egg yolk and then lightly spread the paste over the tops – do not go over the edges.

Bake at 180° C for 30 – 40 minutes or until cooked. Dredge with icing sugar. Reserve your best Port wine to serve with God's Bread.

# Easter Cross Bread
## *Folar da Páscoa*

This is served on Easter Sunday and, again, each region in Portugal has its own version. In some places bread dough is used as the basis to which the rest of the ingredients are added; in other places *chá de ervas* (cinnamon stick, aniseed and fennel boiled in water) is used to flavour the dough.

250 g bread dough (use the recipe for Portuguese rolls on p151)
2 eggs
5 ml baking powder
5 ml ground cinnamon
5 ml aniseed
5 ml grated lemon rind

100 g butter
50 ml warm milk
20 ml *aguardente*
flour

**To decorate**
eggs boiled with onion skins (this gives a lovely brown colour)

Place all the ingredients except the flour in a large bowl and beat until well blended. Add enough flour to form a soft dough. Cover and let it rise. When the dough has risen, knock down and shape into a round cake or cakes. Roll out some thin strips of dough and place on the cake(s) in the shape of a cross. Place an egg (parboiled with onion skins for 5 minutes and left in its shell) in each quarter. Brush with beaten egg and bake at 180° C for 25 – 30 minutes.

### Variation
*Trança da Páscoa:* Add 250 g mixed fruits, nuts and cherries to the dough before shaping. Cut the dough into 3 strips and plait them, or cut into 2 strips and twist them together. Brush with beaten egg and bake at 180° C for 25 – 30 minutes.

# King's Crown Cake
## *Bolo Rei*

This cake is traditionally eaten during Christmas and New Year but in some places it is served only on *Dia de Reis* which falls on 6 January. Just as the Three Kings brought gifts to the baby Jesus, this cake is taken as a gift when visiting friends and family during the festive season. Small gifts – such as charms – are wrapped in foil and placed in the cake before baking. A dried broad bean *(fava)* is also placed in the cake mixture. The person who finds the bean in his or her slice of cake has to pay for the cake the following year. This tradition gives rise to great excitement, not least of which is the speed with which the cake has to be sliced and eaten!

| | |
|---|---|
| 250 g mixed fruits (nuts, raisins, sultanas, pine kernels – a must) | 4 eggs |
| | 100 ml warm milk |
| | pinch of salt |
| 50 ml Port wine | 125 g soft butter |
| 25 g yeast (1 cake) | |
| 5 ml sugar | ***To decorate*** |
| 62 ml warm water | whole glacé fruits |
| 625 g flour | coloured sugar crystals |
| 150 g castor sugar | warmed apricot jam |

Soak the fruit in the Port wine overnight, or for at least 8 – 9 hours. Mix the yeast and 5 ml sugar with the warm water. Sprinkle with 62 ml flour, put in a warm place and allow a sponge to form. It is ready when the flour starts to crack. Place in the bowl of a food mixer and add the rest of the ingredients except the fruit and the butter. Beat well for 5 – 6 minutes, adding the butter little by little. Cover the mixture and allow it to rise until double in size. (This will take 2 – 3 hours, depending on the weather and the temperature in the kitchen.)

When the dough has risen, add the fruit and mix well. Shape the dough into two ring-shaped crowns. Place a greased jam tin in the middle to hold the shape. Brush with egg yolk and decorate with glacé fruit and sugar crystals. Bake at 180° C for 30 – 35 minutes. Remove from the oven and brush with warmed apricot jam.

The above quantities will be enough for 2 cakes, which can be frozen until required.

# Sweet Breads
## *Bolos Doces (Bolos dos Noivos)*

It was customary to bake these cakes for wedding festivities. They were given to friends and neighbours to confirm that they had been invited to the wedding. (If you didn't get a cake, you didn't bother pitching up.)

On the wedding day someone carried a basket, lined with a beautiful white tablecloth, filled with these cakes. As the bride and groom left the church, anyone who greeted them or showered them with flowers was presented with a cake as a thank-you. Can you imagine how many cakes would have to be baked nowadays, when wedding guests can number as many as 500?

This is one of those recipes that has been handed down by my in-laws. I have simplified it, assuming that you are not going to use the cakes as invitations or thank-you cards.

| | |
|---|---|
| 125 ml water | 125 g butter |
| strip of lemon rind | 25 g yeast (1 cake) |
| 10 – 15 g whole aniseed | 5 ml sugar |
| 1 stick cinnamon | 625 g flour |
| 250 ml sugar | |

Boil the water with the lemon rind, aniseed and cinnamon stick for 5 – 10 minutes. Strain. Add the sugar and butter to the water, mix well and allow to cool until lukewarm. Mix the yeast with 5 ml sugar and a little warm water and leave for 5 minutes. Sift the flour. Add the yeast mixture and the lukewarm liquid. Knead to a dough, adding more flour if necessary. Cover and allow to rise until double in size. Shape into small round cakes. Cover and let rise again. Bake at 180° C for 20 – 25 minutes or until nicely brown. Remove from the oven and brush with melted butter.

# Rose Cake

## *Bolo das 7 Rosas*

This is the Portuguese version of Chelsea buns.

| | |
|---|---|
| 15 g yeast | *Filling* |
| 5 ml sugar | 100 g ground almonds |
| 400 g flour | 100 g butter |
| 60 g soft butter | 10 ml grated lemon rind |
| 5 ml ground cinnamon | 150 g sugar |
| 100 ml warm milk | 5 ml ground cinnamon |
| 2 eggs | 50 g nibbed almonds |
| 10 ml grated lemon rind | 10 g pine kernels *(pinhoes)* |
| 50 g sugar | 150 g glacé fruits, finely chopped |

Mix the 5 ml sugar with the yeast to form a paste. Sift the flour, add the yeast mixture, the soft butter, cinnamon, warm milk, eggs, lemon rind and sugar. Knead together to make a soft dough. Cover and allow to rise until double in size.

Make a paste with the ground almonds, butter, lemon rind and sugar. (This is easily done in a food processor.)

Place the dough on a floured board and roll into a rectangle (about 35 by 20 cm). Spread the paste evenly over the dough. Sprinkle with the cinnamon, nibbed almonds, pine kernels and glacé fruit. Roll up (like a Swiss roll) and cut the roll into 7 equal-sized slices. Place the slices in a greased and floured round 25 cm cake tin, with the cut side up – 1 slice in the centre and 6 around the circumference. Cover and let the dough rise again.

Brush with beaten egg and bake at 180° C for 30 – 35 minutes or until cooked.

# Afternoon Cakes
## *Bolos Para Lanche*

After giving you so many recipes that demand that you knead and wait, I decided to include something that is not only traditional but also very quick to make.

3 eggs
250 g sugar
10 ml grated lemon rind
pinch of salt
125 ml olive oil
125 ml cooking oil
250 ml warm milk

750 g flour (more may be needed)
5 ml baking powder
250 g ground almonds
5 ml ground cinnamon
beaten egg
125 ml castor sugar, for sprinkling

Beat the eggs, sugar, lemon rind and salt until light in colour. Add the warmed (finger-hot) oils and milk, beating all the time. Add the sifted flour and baking powder, almonds and cinnamon. Mix well until a dough is formed. Shape into round cakes about the size of a golf ball and place on a greased and floured baking sheet. Brush with beaten egg, sprinkle with castor sugar and bake in a hot oven (200° C) for 30 – 35 minutes.

**As I have explained, making bread is a whole day's work, especially if you have to gather the wood, light the fire and wait for the clay oven to heat up. Many other dishes made from bread dough are baked in the oven at the same time as the bread. The three recipes that follow are examples of these.**

# Bacalhau Pie
## *Bola de Bacalhau*

3 onions, sliced
2 cloves garlic, crushed
125 ml olive oil
250 g *bacalhau*, cooked and
   flaked (see p2)
25 ml chopped parsley

piri piri to taste
salt, if necessary
1 kg bread dough (use the
   recipe for home-made
   bread, p150)
1 egg, beaten

Fry the onions and garlic in the olive oil. Add the fish, parsley and seasonings. Continue frying for a few minutes and then remove from the heat and cool. Grease a deep baking tray (20 by 30 cm) with olive oil. Line the tray with half the dough and spread the fish mixture over it. Roll out the remaining dough and cover the fish with it. Fold the sides of the dough over the top layer to seal. Brush with olive oil and beaten egg. Bake at 200° C for about 1 hour. Serve hot or cold.

**Variations for fillings**
* Stew and debone chicken, and add some of the gravy.
* Use fresh or tinned sardines and lots of onion slices.
* Sliced cold meats, such as *chouriço* or smoked ham.
* Invent some.

# Tuna Fish Bread
## *Bola de Atum*

350 g flour
15 ml baking powder
5 ml salt
3 eggs
500 ml milk
250 ml oil
1 tin tuna, drained

70 ml grated cheese
3 hard-boiled eggs, chopped
150 g pitted olives
100 g chopped tomatoes
15 ml chopped parsley
15 ml chopped onions

Grease a ring tin and dust with flour. Sift the flour, baking powder and salt into a large mixing bowl. Make a well in the centre and add the raw eggs, milk and oil. Beat well. Add all the remaining ingredients and fold in with a metal spoon. (Note: Do not mix after each addition.) Pour into the greased pan and bake at 180° C for 1 hour. Serve hot or cold – ideal for a picnic.

# *Chouriço* Bread
## *Bola de Chouriço*

450 g flour
25 ml baking powder
5 ml salt
4 eggs
250 ml cooking oil
250 ml milk

250 ml *chouriço*, finely
chopped
125 ml fried bacon, finely
chopped
125 ml Cheddar cheese, grated
25 ml chopped fresh herbs
1 egg yolk, beaten
*chouriço* slices for garnishing

Sift the flour, baking powder and salt. Add the eggs, oil and milk and beat well to form a batter. Fold in the *chouriço,* bacon, cheese and herbs. Place in a loaf pan. Brush with beaten egg yolk and garnish with slices of *chouriço.* Bake at 200° C for approximately 1 hour.

**Variation**
Substitute chicken for the *chouriço* and bacon.

# Large Cakes
## *Bolos*

Portuguese housewives love to bake cakes. Recipes are exchanged everywhere – in fisheries, hairdressers, on the bus. I have included only recipes that are very typically Portuguese.

It was the custom for neighbours to send to the home of a bride or groom the eggs, nuts, flour and wine needed for the baking that preceded wedding festivities. A tray of cakes was reserved for those who could not attend the wedding and sent to them later. It is still a tradition today to keep some of the wedding cake for those who were unable to be at the wedding. *Pão de Ló* (sponge cake) was always included on the tray. There must be hundreds of versions of this cake, each named after a place or a person. Some contained as many as 26 eggs! Sponge cake is usually baked in a ring tin, but in some places it is still baked in an earthenware bowl lined with thick paper.

I would like to share with you a recipe for *Pão de Ló* taken from my mother's recipe book dated 1936.

# Pão de Ló de Coimbra

7 eggs
250 g sugar
150 g flour
pinch of salt

Separate the eggs. Beat the egg yolks with the sugar until light. Fold in the beaten egg whites. Sift the flour and the salt and fold lightly into the egg and sugar mixture. Place in a ring tin and bake.

    The recipe gave no indication of oven temperature or baking time. One cannot help but wonder how housewives managed to produce perfect sponge cakes in clay ovens without the advantages of thermometers or thermostats. (If you are not disposed to experiment, try 180° C for about 25 minutes . . . )

# Water Sponge
## Pão de Ló de Água

I prefer this recipe because it uses fewer eggs and the water gives it a light texture.

6 eggs, separated
200 g sugar
5 ml grated lemon rind
50 ml water

150 g flour
pinch of salt
5 ml baking powder

Beat the egg yolks, sugar and lemon rind until thick and pale. Add the water, beating all the time. Fold in the stiffly beaten egg whites. Finally, using a hand whisk, fold in the sifted flour, salt and baking powder. Bake in a greased ring tin at 185° C for 20 – 25 minutes.

# Granny's Spice Cake
## *Bolo Preto da Avó*

This is definitely *Avó's* cake. Although the recipe has been handed down to daughters and granddaughters, no one makes it as well as she did. The spicy flavour improves with time, so make it 2 – 3 days before required and store it in an airtight container.

| | |
|---|---|
| 500 g flour | 250 g melted margarine |
| 400 g brown sugar | grated rind of 1 lemon |
| 15 ml bicarbonate of soda | 250 ml milk |
| pinch of salt | 250 ml milk stout |
| 12 ml cocoa | 4 eggs |
| 12 ml ground cinnamon | 25 ml treacle |
| 2 ml ground cloves | 100 ml Madeira *or* Port wine |
| 5 ml ground nutmeg | |

Sift the dry ingredients. Add the melted margarine and the rest of the ingredients, except the wine. Beat well. Place in a greased ring tin or a large (22 cm) round pan. Bake at 180° C for approximately 45 minutes. Remove from the pan and cool. Drizzle 100 ml Madeira or Port wine over the top of the cake.

# Pineapple Cake
## *Bolo de Ananás*

As the modern housewife gathers new cake recipes, some of the older ones decline in popularity. But this one seems to have survived the years – there is no wedding or christening without pineapple cake.

| | |
|---|---|
| 250 ml sugar for the caramel | 2 eggs |
| 1 large pineapple, cut into | 125 g margarine |
|    rings *or* 1 large tin | 125 ml milk |
|    pineapple rings | 65 ml pineapple juice |
| glacé cherries | 10 ml grated orange rind |
| 375 ml flour | 10 ml baking powder |
| 180 ml sugar | |

Make the caramel by placing the 250 ml sugar in a heavy saucepan and melting over low heat until it turns golden. Line a cake tin (preferably a ring tin) with the caramel. Place the pineapple rings in a circle around the base and sides of the tin. Place a cherry in the centre of each pineapple ring.

Mix all the ingredients, except the baking powder, in a bowl and beat until soft (about 5 minutes using an electric beater). Fold in the baking powder. Carefully pour the mixture into the prepared tin and bake at 180° C for 50 – 60 minutes.

# 'Not-so-fresh' Cake
## *Bolo Podre*

*Podre* means 'not so fresh'. I gather that the name given to this cake derives from its colour (a sort of marbled brown) and not from its taste. The olive oil and honey mixture give it a delicious, quite different flavour.

| | |
|---|---|
| 6 eggs, separated | 80 ml brandy |
| 100 g sugar | 250 g flour |
| 10 ml grated orange rind | pinch of salt |
| 100 ml cooking oil | 5 ml ground cinnamon |
| 100 ml olive oil | 5 ml ground aniseed |
| 300 ml honey | 10 ml baking powder |

Beat the egg yolks with the sugar and orange rind until pale. Slowly add the oils, honey and brandy, beating all the time. Sift the dry ingredients together and fold into the mixture. Lastly, fold in the beaten egg whites. Bake in a ring tin that has been greased and dusted with flour for 50 – 60 minutes at 180° C. Using a skewer, test that the cake is cooked before removing from the oven.

# Madeiran 'Honey' Cake
## *Bolo de Mel da Madeira*

There is not a household in Madeira that does not make this delicious cake at Christmas time. The 'honey' is actually molasses, but locally we use treacle. This is a very rich cake which can be kept for up to a year (if nobody finds it). It is usually baked at the beginning of December.

The cake is never cut with a knife – it is always broken into pieces for serving. I have been unable to discover the reason for this tradition. I once suggested that it could be a custom dating from biblical times, or perhaps it was to prevent the nuts' being sliced, or perhaps it was because knives didn't exist when the cake was first created – the last remark was not appreciated!

| | |
|---|---|
| 1 kg flour | 75 g sultanas |
| 500 g sugar | 100 g mixed peel |
| 25 g bicarbonate of soda | 100 ml grated orange rind |
| 15 g ground cinnamon | 50 ml grated lemon rind |
| 10 g ground cloves | 500 g melted butter |
| 5 ml pepper | 250 ml stout |
| 2 ml salt | 25 ml Madeira wine |
| 5 ml ground ginger | 500 ml treacle |
| 5 ml ground nutmeg | juice of 1 orange |
| 5 ml ground aniseed | |
| 5 ml mixed spice | ***For decoration*** |
| 500 g walnuts, finely chopped | whole walnuts, almonds and |
| 100 g almonds, chopped | cut peel |

Place all the dry ingredients in a large mixing bowl. Make a well in the centre and add the melted butter, stout, wine, treacle and orange juice. Mix until well blended – the mixture should come away from the sides of the bowl. If the mixture is too soft add a little more flour – it should be the consistency of bread dough.

Brush the top of the mixture with a little melted butter, cover and leave overnight. Line loose-bottomed sandwich tins with paper and grease well. Place about 500 g of dough in each tin, and press down well, flattening the top. Decorate with whole walnuts, almonds and pieces of cut peel. In Madeira it is the custom to make very ornate patterns with the nuts and peel, each person trying to outdo the other. I like to arrange strips of almonds to read *Feliz Natal*, which means 'Merry Christmas'.

Bake in a moderate oven (150 – 160° C) for 15 – 20 minutes. Do not let the cakes dry out: they should be cooked but still soft when removed from the oven – test with a toothpick. Leave the cakes in the tins for a while before turning out. Cool and then wrap in cling wrap and store in airtight containers until Christmas.

# Rolls and Tarts
## *Tortas e Tartes*

*Tortas* (Rolls): Portuguese housewives have mastered the art of rolling. Believe me, to roll some of these mixtures successfully you have to work very quickly indeed. Most of the rolls require a deep Swiss-roll tin. I prefer to line the tin with a cooking bag which I grease with cooking spray or brush with melted butter. Have ready a board covered with a wet dish cloth over which you have placed a sheet of greaseproof paper sprinkled with sugar. If rolls are overcooked and dry it will be impossible to roll them. The underneath of the roll may look translucent and uncooked, but it is in fact set.

*Tartes* (Tarts): These are ordinary pastry-lined tarts with interesting fillings.

## Rolls
### *Tortas*

# Carrot Roll
## *Torta de Cenoura*

500 g raw carrots
500 g sugar
40 ml grated orange rind

4 eggs, separated
65 ml flour
15 ml baking powder

Peel and cook the carrots. Mash or blend until smooth. Add the sugar and orange rind and beat well. Add the egg yolks and beat. Fold in the flour and baking powder. Lastly, fold in the beaten egg whites. Pour into a prepared tin and bake at 180° C for 30 minutes, or until firm to the touch. Turn out on to a prepared board (see above) and roll.

Sometimes this roll is filled with *Ovos Moles* (see p185).

**Variation**
*Lençinhos* (Sweet Hankies): Turn out the cake on to the prepared board but do not roll. Instead, cut into squares, spread with *Ovos Moles* (p185) or Confectioner's Custard (p125) and fold into triangles.

# Almond Roll
## *Torta de Amêndoa*

125 g whole almonds in skins
400 g sugar
6 eggs
15 ml butter

Grind the almonds finely. Beat all ingredients together and pour into a prepared tin. Bake in a hot oven (190° C) for 10 – 15 minutes. Turn out on to a prepared board and roll as described above.

# Coconut Roll
## *Torta de Coco*

4 eggs, separated
400 g sugar
10 ml grated lemon rind
150 g butter

150 g desiccated coconut
15 ml cornflour (maizena)
100 g sugar

Mix the egg yolks, sugar, lemon rind and butter until well blended. (Do *not* cream.) Add the coconut and maizena and mix well. Beat the egg whites until stiff, gradually adding 100 g sugar and beating all the time. Fold into the mixture. Pour into a prepared tin and bake at 190° C for 25 – 35 minutes, or until firm to the touch but not dry. Turn out on to a prepared board and roll as described above.

# Honey Roll
## *Torta de Mel*

10 eggs
400 g sugar
25 ml cornflour (maizena)
5 ml ground cinnamon

1 ml ground nutmeg
200 ml honey
450 g melted butter

Mix the eggs with the sugar, maizena, spices and honey. Add the cooled melted butter and mix well. Pour into a greased deep Swiss-roll tin. Bake at 190° C for 20 – 25 minutes. Using a toothpick or skewer, test that the roll is cooked before removing from the oven. Turn out on to a prepared board and roll as described above.

### Variation
If this cake proves difficult to roll, cut it into squares and roll them in chopped nuts – just as delicious!

# Orange Roll
## *Torta de Laranja*

8 eggs
500 g sugar
250 ml orange juice

50 ml cornflour (maizena)
5 ml grated orange rind
5 ml baking powder

Stir eggs and sugar together — do not beat. Mix orange juice and maizena together and then add to egg and sugar mixture. Add the orange rind and baking powder and stir thoroughly. Pour into a Swiss-roll tin lined with a cooking bag. Bake at 200° C for 12 – 15 minutes. Turn out on to a damp cloth dusted with sugar and roll very quickly. Serve cold as a cake or a pudding.

# Chocolate Salami
## *Torta de Chocolate*
## *(Salami de Chocolate)*

Many a time my mother made this roll ahead of time when she was expecting
visitors. And many a time the visitors did not get any of it because we got to it
before they arrived. I need hardly tell you what we got for doing this . . .

30 ml soft butter
200 g sugar
2 eggs

200 g drinking chocolate
   powder
200 g Marie biscuits, crushed

Mix together the butter, sugar, eggs and chocolate and beat lightly. Fold in the
crushed biscuits. If the mixture is too soft place in the refrigerator for a while.
Turn the mixture on to greaseproof paper sprinkled with sugar and shape into
a roll. Wrap in the greaseproof paper and refrigerate until hard. Cut into slices
before serving.

If liked, 50 g nibbed almonds or chopped walnuts may be added to the
mixture.

The above quantities will make two rolls – one for the visitors and one for
the kids.

# Chestnut Salami
## *Salami de Castanhas*

Sweetened chestnut purée may be used if whole chestnuts are not available,
but you should then omit the sugar.

1 kg chestnuts
250 ml milk
150 g almonds, chopped
50 g glacé pineapple, chopped
80 ml drinking chocolate powder

50 g glacé cherries (green and
   red)
50 ml Port wine
100 g soft butter
5 ml grated orange rind
200 g castor sugar

Blanch the chestnuts in boiling water for 10 minutes or until the skin is easily removed. Remove the skins, cut in half and place in a saucepan with the milk and a little water. Simmer until soft, adding more liquid if necessary. Pour into a food processor and blend until smooth. Place the chestnut purée in a bowl, add all the remaining ingredients and mix well. Shape into a roll, wrap in greaseproof paper and store in the refrigerator until required. Cut into slices before serving.

# Chocolate Log
## *Tronco do Natal*

Perhaps not typically Portuguese, but it has a place of honour at the Christmas table.

*Swiss roll*
5 large eggs, separated
100 g sugar
10 ml grated lemon rind
100 g flour

*Filling*
200 g chocolate and hazelnut
  spread

*Chocolate icing*
250 g butter
750 g icing sugar
  (approximately)
60 ml cocoa powder, dissolved
  in a little boiling water
coffee liqueur to taste

Preheat the oven to 180° C. Line a Swiss-roll tin. Beat the egg yolks, sugar and lemon rind until pale. Fold in the beaten egg whites. Lastly, fold in the sifted flour. Pour into the prepared tin and bake for 12 – 15 minutes. Turn out on to a prepared board (see p165), trim the edges, spread with filling and roll. Allow to cool.

*To make the icing:* Beat the butter until soft and then add the icing sugar gradually. Beat until fluffy. Add the cocoa and liqueur and beat well.

*To assemble:* Cut off a quarter of the Swiss roll and then cut this piece in half. Place the larger piece of the roll (the 'log') on a platter or board and arrange the smaller pieces alongside the 'log' to form 'branches'. Spread the icing thickly on the top and sides of both 'log' and 'branches'. Score the iced surface with a fork so that it resembles bark. If you are feeling adventurous, place the icing in an icing bag fitted with a star nozzle and cover the 'log' and 'branches'. Decorate with holly leaves.

# Bridal Pillow
## *Travesseiro de Noiva*

You must be expert at rolling by now, so go ahead and try rolling this one . . .

| | |
|---|---|
| 10 egg whites | *Sauce (Ovos Moles)* |
| 220 g sugar | 7 egg yolks |
| | 300 g sugar |
| | 150 ml water |

Prepare the sauce *(Ovos Moles)* following the recipe on p185 before making the roll.

Grease a deep Swiss-roll tin or line it with a cooking bag. Beat the egg whites until stiff. Add the sugar gradually, beating all the time. Spoon into the prepared tin and bake in a very hot oven (190° C) for 8 – 10 minutes. Remove from the oven and cool for 1 minute. Turn out on to greased greaseproof paper and very carefully spread half the sauce over the surface. Roll very lightly. Cool. Pour the remaining sauce over the roll just before serving.

# Tarts
## *Tartes*

# Almond and Caramel Tart
## *Picado de Abelha*

Use a large, shallow, loose-bottomed fluted baking tin. Or double the quantities and bake in a deep tray and cut into squares.

| | |
|---|---|
| 6 eggs | *Topping* |
| 200 g soft butter | 200 g sugar |
| pinch of salt | 200 g butter |
| 200 g sugar | 250 g chopped or slivered |
| 200 g flour | almonds |
| 100 g ground almonds | 100 ml milk |
| 2 ml baking powder | |
| milk | |

Place all the ingredients for the tart, except the milk, in a bowl and beat together for 5 minutes. If necessary, add a little milk to make a soft consistency. Spread into a greased baking tin.

Next, make the topping. Place the sugar, butter and almonds in a saucepan and, watching very carefully to see that it does not burn, bring to the boil. Continue cooking until a caramel is formed. Add the milk very carefully, stirring all the time. Pour the topping over the dough in the greased baking tin and bake at 180° C for 25 – 30 minutes.

# Chick Pea Tart
## *Tarte de Grão*

1 packet ready-to-use puff
   or shortcrust pastry

*Filling*
250 g sugar
3 whole eggs

3 egg yolks
15 ml grated lemon rind
160 g cooked and finely
   mashed chick peas
75 ml melted butter
icing sugar for dredging

Line a pie dish with the pastry and prick with a fork. Beat the sugar, whole eggs, egg yolks and lemon rind together and add the chick pea purée. Mix in the melted butter. Pour into the pastry shell and bake at 180° C for 35 – 40 minutes. Dust with icing sugar when cold.

# Small Tarts and Pastries
## *Pastéis*

## *Pastéis de Nata*

These tartlets, also known as *Pastéis de Belem*, after the place where they originated, are a true Portuguese delicacy. You must have a very hot oven to make these successfully.

1 packet ready-to-use puff
  pastry

*Filling*
9 egg yolks

10 ml flour
500 ml cream
150 ml sugar
2 ml grated lemon rind
  (optional)

Roll out the pastry thinly. Cut into strips about 14 cm wide and roll the strips like a Swiss-roll. Cut the rolls into 'wheels', 2 – 3 cm wide. Place the pastry wheels in greased patty tins. Dip your thumb in cold water and press the pastry wheels so that they line the tins. Refrigerate while preparing the filling.

Beat the egg yolks. Add the flour, mixed with a little milk. Add the cream and sugar and mix well. Place in a saucepan and bring to the boil. Add the lemon rind. Remove from the heat and cool slightly. Pour into a jug. Pour the filling into the pastry-lined tins until three-quarters full.

Bake in a very hot oven (300° C) until golden brown with a dark, almost black, centre (15 – 20 minutes). Some people like to sprinkle ground cinnamon over the cooked tartlets.

## Bean Tarts
## *Pastéis de Feijão*

1 packet ready-to-use puff
  or shortcrust pastry
icing sugar for dredging

*Filling*
300 g cooked and puréed haricot
  beans

6 egg yolks
2 whole eggs
125 g ground almonds
500 g sugar
250 ml water

Line small patty tins with the pastry. Mix the bean purée, egg yolks, whole eggs and ground almonds in a bowl. Mix the sugar and water in a saucepan over a low heat and when the sugar has dissolved boil for 5 minutes. Cool, and then pour the syrup slowly over the bean mixture, stirring all the time. Spoon the mixture into the pastry-lined tins and bake at 220° C for 15 – 20 minutes. Cool and sprinkle with icing sugar.

# Almond Tarts
## *Pastéis de Amêndoa*

The method for making these tartlets is the same as that given above for Bean Tarts – only the ingredients differ.

| | |
|---|---|
| 1 packet ready-to-use puff pastry | 150 g ground almonds |
| | 50 g finely chopped almonds |
| | 30 g butter |
| *Filling* | 6 egg yolks |
| 300 g sugar | 2 whole eggs |
| 150 ml water | 15 ml grated lemon rind |

Make a syrup with the sugar and water. Mix all the remaining ingredients together and pour the syrup over them, stirring all the time. Fill pastry-lined patty tins and bake.

# Tartlets Sintra-style
## *Queijadas de Sintra*

In Portugal these tartlets are made with *queijo fresco*.

| | |
|---|---|
| 1 packet ready-to-use shortcrust pastry | 250 ml castor sugar |
| | 350 g cream cheese |
| | pinch of ground cinnamon |
| *Filling* | 4 egg yolks |
| 25 g soft butter | 125 ml flour |

Cream together the butter, castor sugar and cream cheese. Add the cinnamon. Add the egg yolks one at a time, beating well after each addition. Fold in the sifted flour. Chill the filling for a couple of hours. Line patty tins with the pastry and half-fill with the cream cheese mixture. Bake in a very hot oven (220° C) for about 15 minutes.

# Coconut Tartlets
## *Pastéis de Coco*

1 packet ready-to-use
   shortcrust or puff pastry
icing sugar for dusting

*Filling*
400 g sugar

200 ml water
200 g desiccated coconut
2 ml grated lemon rind
4 egg yolks
5 whole eggs

Make a syrup with the sugar and water: dissolve the sugar in the water over low heat, bring to the boil and simmer for 4 minutes. Remove from heat and allow to cool slightly. Add the coconut and lemon rind, mix well and allow to cool completely. Meanwhile, line patty tins with the pastry.

Add the eggs yolks and the whole eggs to the coconut mixture and mix well. Spoon into the pastry-lined patty tins, dust with icing sugar and bake at 190° C for 25 – 30 minutes, or until golden brown.

# Tartlets from Bahia
## *Quindins da Baia*

4 eggs
100 ml sugar
125 ml desiccated coconut

20 ml coconut milk (see p125)
20 ml melted butter

Beat the eggs and add the remaining ingredients. Spoon into greased patty tins and bake in a bain-marie in a hot oven (185° C) for 20 minutes. Unmould and place in paper cases. The crust that forms on the top during baking will be the base of each unmoulded tartlet. The top of each tartlet will have a custard-like texture.

# Potato Tartlets

## *Bolinhos de Batata*

This is another of my mother's specialities, taken from her collection and only slightly adapted by me.

| | |
|---|---|
| 250 g mashed potatoes | 5 ml baking powder |
| 2 eggs | 15 ml flour |
| 250 g castor sugar | 20 ml soft butter |
| 10 ml grated lemon rind | |

Beat all the ingredients together and spoon into greased patty pans. Bake at 180° C for 15 – 20 minutes, or until set.

# Tentúgal Rolls

## *Pastéis de Tentúgal*

Every time I visited Portugal these tarts were at the top of my list of delicacies to be savoured. The recipe had always seemed too long and complicated to contemplate making them. But when I eventually took the time to re-read the recipe carefully, I discovered that there was nothing complicated at all. As a matter of fact they are very easy to make, provided you can obtain ready-made phyllo pastry.

| | |
|---|---|
| ready-made phyllo pastry | *Filling:* Ovos Moles |
| 100 g melted butter | 250 g sugar |
| icing sugar for dusting | 10 egg yolks |
| | 100 ml water |

Make the *Ovos Moles* according to the recipe on p185. Cut the pastry into rectangular pieces measuring about 12 x 10 cm. Layer 6 sheets of pastry one on top of the other, brushing each sheet with melted butter before adding the next one. Keep the pastry covered with a damp cloth while working.

Place about 10 ml of *Ovos Moles* on the pastry and roll it, folding the ends up like a parcel. Bake in a hot oven (200° C) for 10 – 12 minutes. Sprinkle with icing sugar when cooked.

# Small Cakes and Biscuits
## *Bolinhos e Bolachas*

# Iced Popovers
## *Cavacas*

If you have time, look through the glass door of your oven and watch how popovers turn over in their tins.

| | |
|---|---|
| 1 egg | *Royal icing* |
| 15 ml olive oil (*or* 7,5 ml | 1 egg white |
| cooking oil + 7,5 ml olive oil) | 2 ml lemon juice |
| pinch of salt | icing sugar |
| 15 ml flour | |
| 20 ml brandy | |
| olive oil for greasing tins | |

These are the basic ingredients. You may double, or even triple, the quantities if you wish.

Place all the ingredients in a bowl and beat for 15 – 20 minutes. (I advise you to use an electric beater.) Brush muffin pans with lots of olive oil. Place a tablespoon of the mixture in each muffin tin. Bake in a very hot oven (200° C) for 10 – 15 minutes, and then reduce the heat to 180° C and continue baking for a further 20 minutes (or until the popovers have flipped). Brush with royal icing when cool.

*To make the royal icing:* Beat the egg white and lemon juice slightly. Add sifted icing sugar slowly, beating all the time. Continue adding icing sugar until the mixture forms and holds peaks.

# Rice Cakes
## *Bolos de Arroz*

These are baked in special rings lined with a strip of paper which is not removed after baking. The name of the bakery or confectioner is usually printed on the paper. Make your own rings by removing the top and bottom of a shallow tin (such as a tuna fish tin) and line it with greaseproof paper. Grease the paper well. For children's parties write the name of each child on the strips of paper before lining the rings.

| | |
|---|---|
| 100 g butter *or* margarine | 200 g rice flour |
| 250 g sugar | pinch of salt |
| 5 ml grated lemon rind | 5 ml baking powder |
| 3 eggs, separated | 150 ml milk (approximately) |
| 200 g flour | sugar for sprinkling |

Line the rings as described above and place on a greased baking tray. (If rings are unobtainable, use muffin tins.) Cream the butter or margarine, sugar and lemon rind together and then add the egg yolks one at a time. Sift together the flour, rice flour, salt and baking powder and stir into the creamed mixture alternately with the milk. Fold in the beaten egg whites. Spoon the mixture into the rings until they are two-thirds full. Sprinkle with sugar and bake in a hot oven (180° C) for 20 – 25 minutes. Remove from the rings and cut off any spill-overs.

# Sighs (Meringues)
## *Suspiros*

After beating dozens of egg whites by hand for hours, what else do you do but sigh? But after baking them to perfection, the sigh is one of relief and pleasure.

4 egg whites
pinch of cream of tartar
250 g sugar
5 ml grated lemon rind

The egg whites should be at room temperature. Separate the eggs very carefully because the slightest trace of yolk will prevent the whites from beating properly. Bowls and beaters must be extremely clean.

Place the egg whites and cream of tartar in a bowl and beat until peaks form. Gradually add half the sugar, beating all the time. Fold in the remaining sugar and the grated lemon rind with a metal spoon.

Pipe or spoon the meringue on to greased baking trays or trays lined with baking paper. Bake in a very cool oven (100° C) for 2 – 3 hours.

**Variation**
Cut the cooked meringues open and fill with *Ovos Moles* (see p185).

# Carriços

This is one of the specialities of S. Brás de Alportel, my hometown.

| | |
|---|---|
| 4 egg whites | 2 ml lemon juice |
| 250 g sugar | 250 g toasted slivered almonds |
| 10 ml grated lemon rind | whole almonds cut in half |

Beat the egg whites until stiff. Add the sugar gradually and beat until peaks form. Add the lemon rind and lemon juice, and fold in the slivered almonds. Place in spoonfuls on a greased baking tray. Place half an almond in the centre of each. Bake in a cool oven (120° C) for 1 – 1 $^1/_2$ hours.

**Variation**
Substitute chopped walnuts for the almonds – and call it your own speciality.

# Beer Twists
## *Palitos de Cerveja*

| | |
|---|---|
| 200 g soft butter | *Coating* |
| 450 g flour | egg white |
| 75 ml beer | sugar |

Combine the butter, flour and beer to form a soft dough. Shape into twists, sticks, rings, etc. Dip into lightly beaten egg white and sugar. Place on a greased baking sheet and bake at 190° C for 10 – 15 minutes.

# Treacle Biscuits
## *Broas de Mel da Madeira*

| | |
|---|---|
| 500 g flour | 10 ml grated orange rind |
| 250 g sugar | 10 ml grated lemon rind |
| 10 ml ground cinnamon | 250 g margarine |
| 5 ml ground nutmeg | 3 eggs |
| 15 ml bicarbonate of soda | 250 ml treacle |

Mix all the dry ingredients together. Add the rinds, melted margarine, eggs and treacle. Beat well. Add a little more flour if necessary. Shape into small nut-size biscuits and place on a greased tray. Bake at 190° C for about 10 minutes.

# Sweet Potato and Mealie Meal Biscuits

## *Broas Castelares*

250 g mashed sweet potatoes
250 g sugar
250 g ground almonds
15 ml grated orange rind
15 ml grated lemon rind

125 g flour
125 g mealie meal
50 ml fresh breadcrumbs
4 eggs

Place the mashed potatoes, sugar, ground almonds and rinds in a saucepan. Bring to the boil, stirring continuously. Remove from the heat and add the flour, mealie meal, breadcrumbs and beaten eggs. Mix well. Place on a floured board and allow to cool. Mould portions of the mixture into boat-shaped biscuits, 5 – 6 cm in length. Brush with beaten egg. Sprinkle hundreds-and-thousands over some of the biscuits. Bake in a hot oven (190° C) for 10 – 15 minutes. If wished, the biscuits can be placed on rice paper before baking.

# Tea Biscuits

## *Bolachas do Tio Pedro*

My maternal grandfather and uncles lived in Argentina for many years. They brought back with them the custom of drinking tea *(matte)* in the afternoon. The tea was poured into a calabash-type holder and sipped through a metal straw. Only one calabash was used, so you ate biscuits while you waited for your turn for tea. This was one of the occasions when you were happy to be a child: you were the last to be served with tea but you made up for it by eating large quantities of biscuits while you waited.

My mother used to make large batches of these tea biscuits, and guess who used to help?

250 g soft butter *or* margarine
4 eggs
250 g sugar

10 ml vanilla essence
750 g flour
15 ml baking powder

Combine all the ingredients to make a soft biscuit dough. Roll out and cut into shapes. Place on a greased baking sheet and bake at 180° C for 10 – 15 minutes or until golden.

# Iced Biscuits
## *Bolos de Gema, Bolos Caiados*

2 whole eggs
2 egg yolks
125 g sugar

5 – 10 ml grated lemon rind
90 – 100 ml flour

Whisk the whole eggs and egg yolks with the sugar until pale and light. Add the lemon rind and enough flour to make a soft dough (like beaten cream). Place spoonfuls of the mixture on a greased baking sheet – place them well apart because they spread – and bake at 190° C for 10 minutes. Remove from the baking sheet while hot. When cold, brush on both sides with royal icing (see recipe on p176). Allow to dry on a cake cooler before storing.

# Almond Biscuits
## *Pedrinhas*

150 g butter
90 g sugar
3 egg yolks
1 drop almond essence

50 g ground almonds
10 ml baking powder
150 g flour (approximately)
200 g nibbed almonds

Beat the butter and sugar until creamy. Add the egg yolks and almond essence and beat well. Add the ground almonds and baking powder and enough flour to obtain a biscuit dough. Shape the dough into nut-size balls and roll in the nibbed almonds. Place on a greased baking sheet and bake at 190° C for 20 – 25 minutes.

# My Mother's Favourite Biscuits
## *Biscoitos da Mama*

This is from my mother's 1936 recipe collection. I have substituted cooking oil for some of the olive oil in the original recipe.

| | |
|---|---|
| 3 eggs | *Coating* |
| 25 ml olive oil | 200 g sugar |
| 25 ml cooking oil | 50 ml water |
| 10 ml grated lemon rind | |
| pinch of salt | |
| 300 g flour (approximately) | |

Whisk the eggs with the oils until light and foamy. Add the lemon rind, salt and enough flour (approximately 300 g) to make a soft dough. Knead well. Grease the hands with a little olive oil and form pieces of the dough into finger-shaped biscuits. Place slightly apart on a greased baking tray and bake at 190° C for 20 – 25 minutes.

Place the sugar and water for the coating in a large saucepan. Bring to the boil and simmer until just about to change colour. Remove from the heat and very quickly pour in the cooked biscuits. Using two wooden spoons toss the biscuits in the syrup until they are coated. Separate them and place them on a cooling rack.

# Almond Cakes
## *Bolinhos de Amêndoa*

| | |
|---|---|
| 500 g ground almonds | 1 egg white (reserve the yolk |
| 400 g sugar |    for brushing) |
| 15 ml soft butter | 5 ml baking powder |
| 1 whole egg | |

Mix all the ingredients together to form a dough. Roll portions of the dough into little cakes. Press the centre of each cake with your finger and brush the dent thus formed with lightly beaten egg yolk. Place on greased trays and bake at 160° C until golden brown.

# 'Rich and Famous'

The following delicacies are so rich that they have become famous. Most of them originated in convents or monasteries, hence names like 'Nuns' Tummies', 'Priests' Ears', 'Double-chinned Angels', and they were served to guests after musical evenings. Nowadays we make them for special occasions and I advise you to serve *very* small portions. Some of them contain little more than eggs and sugar – the basic ingredients of most Portuguese sweets.

# Secret Cake
## *Bolo Segredo*

The recipe for this cake was a carefully guarded secret for many years. Now that the secret is out, let us all enjoy it!

6 eggs, separated
300 g sugar
30 ml flour
15 ml melted butter

250 ml *gila* (pumpkin jam, see
    recipe on p192)
350 g ground almonds

Beat all the egg yolks and 3 of the egg whites with the sugar until light. Fold in the flour, melted butter, jam and almonds. Mix well. Beat the remaining 3 egg whites and fold them into the mixture. Pour into a greased 20 cm cake tin. Bake at 180° C until firm to the touch. (The exact cooking time remains a secret!)

# Almond Cake
## *Bolo de Amêndoa*

350 g sugar
150 g ground almonds
150 g mashed potatoes

50 g butter
6 eggs, separated
10 ml grated lemon rind

Mix together the sugar, almonds, potatoes and butter. Add the 6 egg yolks one at a time, beating well after each addition. Add the lemon rind. Fold in 3 beaten egg whites. Pour into a greased and floured 20 cm cake tin and bake at 180° C for 30 – 35 minutes, or until firm to the touch.

# Celestial Cake
## *Toucinho do Céu*

The literal translation of the Portuguese name is 'bacon from heaven'. The cake is certainly heavenly, but the bacon part I cannot figure out at all.

There are hundreds of versions of this recipe – I suppose they all come from heaven.

| | |
|---|---|
| 500 g sugar | 8 egg yolks |
| 250 ml water | 2 ml ground cinnamon |
| 200 g ground almonds | icing sugar for dusting |
| 5 whole eggs | |

Dissolve the sugar in the water. Bring to the boil, stirring continuously, and simmer over low heat for 5 minutes. Add the ground almonds, stir well and remove from heat. Beat the whole eggs and the egg yolks in a bowl. Add the syrup slowly, stirring all the time. Add the cinnamon. Pour the mixture back into the saucepan and, stirring continuously, simmer until it thickens and comes away from the sides of the pan. Pour into a buttered loaf tin and bake at 190° C for 15 – 20 minutes. Dust with icing sugar when cool.

# Egg Threads
## *Fios de Ovos*

This is a most unusual combination of eggs and syrup. There is a special utensil for making the threads. It consists of a small can with three or more pointed spouts or funnels protruding from its base. In the absence of this special utensil, use a pastry bag fitted with a small nozzle. (It will take you the best part of a week to make half a kilogram of threads.) These threads are the basis of many desserts and sweets. They are also used for decorating cakes and hand-made sweets, and can be eaten on their own as well.

12 egg yolks
1 whole egg
1 kg sugar
500 ml water

Place a sieve over a bowl. Place the egg yolks and the whole egg in the sieve and, without beating or pressing, allow the eggs to sift through into the bowl. Make a syrup with the sugar and water: dissolve the sugar in the water, bring to the boil and simmer for 8 – 10 minutes. Reduce the heat.

Pour the sifted eggs into the special spouted utensil (or pastry bag) and drop some of the mixture into the hot syrup with a rotating movement. Cook the threads in the syrup for a minute, then remove the threads with a slotted spoon, rinse in cold water and place in a colander to drain.

Repeat this process until all the egg liquid has been used. If the syrup becomes too thick, thin it with a little water. Separate the threads with the help of two forks dipped in cold water. The syrup may be re-used.

# Soft Eggs
## *Ovos Moles*

Without doubt one of the best known and most popular of all Portuguese sweets, *Ovos Moles* is a traditional delicacy from the northern coastal town of Aveiro where it is sold in little wooden barrels or in shell-shaped wafers. It is used as a filling in almond sweets, rolls, meringues, cakes and pastries. Rice water and rice flour are sometimes added for flavour.

| | |
|---|---|
| 250 g sugar | 30 g rice flour |
| 150 ml water | 8 egg yolks |

Dissolve the sugar in the water and bring to the boil. Simmer until the syrup reaches the 'thread' stage. (Take a spoonful of syrup and tip it out over a dish. If the syrup forms a fine thin thread as it drops into the dish, it has reached the thread stage.) Mix the rice flour with a little water and add it to the syrup. Remove from heat and cool slightly. Pour the syrup over the beaten egg yolks. Return the mixture to the saucepan and simmer until thick, stirring continuously.

*Note:* The number of egg yolks used in the making of *Ovos Moles* may be increased or decreased, depending on the consistency required for a particular recipe.

### Variations
\* If a caramel flavour is required, boil the sugar and water until just beginning to caramelise. Add a little water to cool the syrup and then proceed as above.

\* After adding the eggs to the syrup, add a little Port or Madeira wine and whisk rapidly while cooking. This will give you a foamy sauce which is delicious with Molotov Pudding (see p138).

# Nuns' Tummies
## *Barriga de Freira*

The name of this dish is surely an indication that a sense of humour was not lacking in convent life!

|                        |                          |
|------------------------|--------------------------|
| 250 g sugar            | 5 ml ground cinnamon     |
| 150 ml water           | 35 g butter              |
| 200 g fresh breadcrumbs | 9 egg yolks             |
| 5 ml grated lemon rind | 100 ml sugar (for caramel) |

Dissolve the sugar in the water, bring to the boil and simmer until the 'soft-ball' stage is reached. (Drop a spoonful of the syrup into a bowl of iced water. Using your fingers, mould the syrup in the water into a ball. Remove it from the water. If it immediately loses shape and flattens between your fingers, the syrup is at the soft-ball stage.) Add the breadcrumbs, rind, cinnamon and butter and stir well. Remove from the heat. Add the lightly beaten egg yolks and return to the heat for just long enough to cook the eggs (2 – 3 minutes), stirring all the time. Pour into a serving dish. Make a caramel by placing 100 ml sugar in a heavy saucepan and melting over low heat until it turns golden. Pour the caramel over the 'tummy'.

# Double-chinned Angels
## *Papos de Anjo*

|                |                          |
|----------------|--------------------------|
| 8 egg yolks    | strip of lemon rind      |
| 1 egg white    | strip of orange rind     |
| 500 g sugar    | 1 stick cinnamon         |
| 250 ml water   | naartjie liqueur (optional) |

Whisk the egg yolks and egg white until light and foamy. Pour into well-greased patty tins and bake at 180° C for 15 – 20 minutes. (They are sometimes baked in a bain-marie.) Make a syrup by boiling together the sugar, water, rinds and cinnamon stick for 6 – 7 minutes. Add the liqueur. Soak the baked cakes in the hot syrup until drenched. Place them on a large serving plate and pour more syrup over them.

# Abrantes' Straw
## *Palha de Abrantes*

If a person has a healthy appetite, which is very common among the Portuguese, he is often told to 'go and eat straw in Abrantes'. How lucky can you get? This is truly delicious.

Make a rich *Ovos Moles* (p185), adding 50 g ground almonds, and cook until thick. Pour into a serving dish and decorate with bundles of Egg Threads (p183) (the straw!). Sprinkle with cinnamon.

# Jams and Preserves
*Conservas*
*Doces e Salgadas*

Although we Portuguese definitely have a sweet

tooth, we are not very fond of jams.

The most popular are 'quince cheese' *(Marmelada)*

and pumpkin or squash jam *(Doce de Gila)*.

# Quince Cheese
## *Marmelada*

Quinces are abundant in Portugal. They may be baked in the oven with Port wine, sugar and cinnamon and served as a dessert, but are mostly used for the making of jam. This particular jam has the consistency of cheese and is cut into slices rather than spread. You have the choice of a pale-coloured jam *(Marmelada Branca)* or a jam that is golden-red in colour *(Marmelada Vermelha)*. *Marmelada* served with cottage cheese as a starter is unforgettable.

## *Marmelada Branca*

1 kg quince pulp
1 kg sugar
500 ml liquid (reserve the water in which the quinces are boiled)

Wash the quinces thoroughly. Cover with water and boil the whole, unpeeled quinces until soft (15 – 20 minutes). Drain and reserve the water. When cold enough to handle, peel and remove the pips using your hands or a *wooden* knife. Keep the skins and pips for quince jelly (p193). Mash the quinces. If a smooth jam is required, push the quinces through a very fine sieve.

Dissolve the sugar in the 500 ml liquid and then bring to the boil. Boil for 7 – 8 minutes. Add the quince pulp and reduce the heat. Simmer until thick, stirring all the time. Place in glass ovenproof bowls or trays, cover with a tea shower and dry in the sun for 7 – 8 days, or until a crust has formed on top. (Because we have rain in summer and I don't like taking chances, rather than take the jam outside, I look for a sunny spot in the dining-room or lounge and leave it there.) Cover with greaseproof paper that has been cut to the shape of the container and dipped in Portuguese brandy *(aguardente)*.

## *Marmelada Vermelha*

The lovely colour is produced by allowing the fruit to oxidise. Peel and cut the quinces (now you can use a metal knife) and remove the pips. (Reserve the peel and pips for quince jelly – p193.) Cover the cut fruit with water and boil until soft. Drain and mash the quinces until they are smooth. Weigh the pulp. Place it in a saucepan and add 1 kg sugar for each kg of fruit pulp. Add a cinnamon stick and bring to the boil, stirring all the time. Do be careful when it starts to boil as the mixture tends to splash and can give you a nasty burn (believe me!).

Proceed as for *Marmelada Branca* above.

# Guava Jam
## *Goiabada*

This is a delicious Brazilian jam made in the same way as *marmelada* but using guavas instead of quinces. It is also served sliced.

Peel the guavas and remove the seeds with a teaspoon. Cover with water and boil until the fruit is soft. Proceed as for *Marmelada Branca* or *Marmelada Vermelha* above.

The same recipe can be used for apples and pears: *Maçãnada* will be 'apple cheese' and *Perada* will be 'pear cheese'.

# Grape and Quince Jam
## *Bagulhada*

It is many years since I have made this delicious unusual jam (watching my figure!). It brings back memories of our family's brief sojourn in the Alentejo province.

    2 kg grapes
    250 g peeled, cored and sliced quinces
    1 kg sugar
    200 g chopped walnuts

Wash the grapes and remove the pips (what are children for?). Place in a saucepan and simmer without water for 1 hour. Add the quinces and the sugar and boil for 15 – 20 minutes, or until a fine thread is formed when a small amount of cooled syrup is pulled between thumb and forefinger. Add the chopped nuts, bring to the boil and bottle.

# Brother John's Delights
## *Delicias de Frei João*

This jam is a speciality of the monks at the monastery of Alcobaça. It uses all the sorts of fruit available during the summer: grapes, peeled and seeded (get the neighbours to help this time), melon and quinces are a must. Other fruits can include peaches, apples, etc.

> 1 kg mixed fresh fruit (peeled weight)
> 750 g sugar for each kg of fruit
> 65 g chopped walnuts for each kg of fruit

Peel, core or seed and cut the fruit into small pieces. Place in a large saucepan with the sugar and simmer until thick, stirring occasionally. Add the walnuts and bring to the boil once more. Store in jars or bowls.

# Pumpkin Jam
## *Doce de Gila (Chila)*

*Gila* is a marrow which resembles a large water melon. It is creamy-white inside and the flesh is like threads of spaghetti. It is grown locally by Portuguese market gardeners who call it *Tanarifa*, *Moganga* or *Boganga*. In Madeira it is used in soups but on the Continent it is used to make a most unusual thread-like jam which was a favourite with nuns – hence its use in many of the sweets. It is important to follow the instructions carefully to ensure a successful jam.

*Do not* use any metal utensils to cut the marrow. Smash it into pieces by throwing it on the kitchen floor (how lovely!), pick up the chunks and discard all seeds and any yellow strings around them – these will give the jam a fishy taste.

> *gila*
> sugar
> a few strips of lemon rind
> 300 ml water

Boil the chunks of *gila* in water until the skins come away from the flesh. Drain. Using your hands, peel off the skins and separate the flesh into threads.

Place the threads in a bowl of water as you work. Drain and then place in a bowl of salted water and leave for 24 hours. Change the water twice during this period. Rinse well and then soak in plain water for 24 hours. Drain well, squeezing out all the water. Weigh the *gila* (you should have about 500 g). Place an equal weight of sugar in a saucepan, add the water and bring to the boil. Add the lemon rind and continue boiling for 5 – 6 minutes. Place the *gila* threads in the syrup and continue cooking until thick. Bottle in sterilised jars.

# Chou-chou Jam
## *Doce de Chu-chus*

This is a very easy jam to make and can easily be substituted for *Doce de Gila*. The taste is very similar – if not better.

| | |
|---|---|
| 1 kg ripe chou-chou | 10 ml grated lemon rind |
| 750 g sugar | 125 ml water |
| 10 ml grated orange rind | |

Cut the chou-chou in half and soak them in water for 30 minutes. Drain and then peel and grate the chou-chou coarsely (easy in a food processor). Place the chou-chou in a saucepan with all the other ingredients. Bring to the boil and then simmer until thick, stirring continuously. Bottle and use as required.

# Quince Jelly
## *Geleia de Marmelos*

Place the skins and pips left over from making *Marmelada* in a saucepan with 2 whole quinces and a little water or liquid left over from cooking the quinces. Simmer until the fruit is soft. Strain carefully through a muslin cloth. Do not press or squeeze the cloth as this will result in a cloudy jelly. Measure the strained liquid. Place in a saucepan and add 1 kg sugar for each litre of liquid. Dissolve the sugar in the liquid and bring it to the boil. Remove the scum that rises to the surface, but do not stir. Simmer until thick and then add 5 ml lemon juice.

To test whether the jelly is ready, place a spoonful of jelly in a saucer and allow it to cool. Then draw your finger across the surface of the jelly – if it crinkles, it is ready. Pour the jelly into sterilised jars and seal with wax or greaseproof paper dipped into brandy.

Pieces of cooked quince may be added to the jelly, if liked.

# Tomato Jam
## *Doce de Tomate*

We not only use tomatoes in just about everything, we also make them into jam! Tomato Jam follows *Marmelada* in the popularity polls. Use very ripe tomatoes for the best results.

    1,5 kg tomatoes
    1 kg sugar
    1 stick cinnamon
    15 ml lemon juice

Blanch the tomatoes in boiling water, skin them and remove as many seeds as you can. Cut them into pieces and place them in a colander to drain. Place the drained tomatoes, sugar and cinnamon stick in a large saucepan. Bring to the boil and simmer until thick. To test whether the jam is ready, place a spoonful on a saucer and let it cool. If it crinkles when a finger is drawn over it, it is ready. Add the lemon juice and bring back to the boil. Bottle in sterilised jars.

# Red Pepper Paste
## *Massa de Pimento*
## *(Calda de Pimento)*

My father recalls being paid the equivalent of half a cent for mincing the paste (20 to 25 kilograms at a time). When I came along my grandmother paid me the equivalent of 25 cents, and we did it all by hand, using an old-fashioned mincer (children didn't moan in those days!). With the invention of the food processor my mother, like me, was able to do all the mincing herself, and very quickly too, without having to pay anyone . . .

    The red pepper season in Portugal is short, and this paste is made so that it can be used throughout the year. Because it is very salty, use it sparingly, or reduce the amount of salt in the recipe. Use it in marinades and stews or whenever the taste of peppers is required. It is one of the seasonings used in the making of *linguiça* and *chouriço*.

    10 – 12 red peppers
    250 ml coarse salt (approximately)

Cut the red peppers in half, seed them and slit them so that they are completely flat. Place a layer of red peppers in a bowl (earthenware if possible) and sprinkle with salt. Repeat the layers until you have used up all the peppers. After a day or two a brine will form. Place a heavy object over the top of the peppers so that they are immersed in the brine. Leave for 5 – 6 days. Drain the peppers, wash lightly and place them on a large cake cooler to drain. Dry lightly and then mince the peppers into a paste. Place the paste in jars, leaving a space at the top. Fill the space with olive oil, seal the jars and store them either in the pantry or refrigerator.

**Variation**
Garlic enthusiasts can add some cloves of garlic and a little olive oil during the mincing process.

# Lupins
## *Tremoços*

If, after eating a ton of *tremoços*, you wonder why you can still carry on eating them, read on . . .

Legend has it that while Mary was travelling to Bethlehem she hid behind a large lupin bush. The bush was rather dry and full of seeds and made a rustling noise as Mary moved. She became very annoyed and told it: 'You will never fill any bellies' . . .

The way to eat lupins is first of all to take a handful in your left hand. Then, taking the lupins one at a time between the thumb and forefinger of your right hand, bring them to your mouth, bite the tip to break the skin and with a clicking movement of finger and thumb pop the flesh into your mouth, leaving the skin in your fingers. Can you think of a better party game? Try not to eat the skins as they tend to swell in the tummy.

Ready-to-eat lupins may be bought in glass jars or vacuum packs. Preparing your own takes time and patience.

Pour boiling water over dried lupins and leave to soak overnight. Cook in salted water until tender – it takes about 20 minutes. Drain and place in a large bowl. Cover with cold water and soak for 2 – 3 days changing the water twice daily, or place the bowl under running water. This removes the bitter taste. In Portugal lupins are placed in sacks which are secured to river banks and lowered into the river water. To store lupins, place them in salted water in the refrigerator. When you are ready to serve them, drain and rinse them and sprinkle them with coarse salt.

# Savoury Carrots
## *Conserva de Cenouras*

500 g carrots
125 ml black or green olives

*Dressing*
25 ml olive oil
10 ml sweet paprika

25 ml white wine vinegar
3 cloves garlic, chopped
12,5 ml chopped parsley
1 bay leaf
piri piri to taste
salt and pepper to taste

Boil the carrots whole in salted water. Cut into slices and place in a bowl. Mix together all the ingredients for the dressing, add to the carrots and toss lightly. Add the olives. Refrigerate until required.

# Olives
## *Azeitonas*

Green olives are available locally in season. It is fun to prepare your own, so go ahead and make your friends envious.

# Crushed Olives
## *Azeitonas Britadas*

Gently crush olives with a stone, but do not break the pips. Place in a bowl and cover with water. Soak for 12 – 15 days, changing the water every day. This will remove the bitterness. Taste as you go along – it might take less time. Place in brine with lemon slices, garlic and oregano and use within a month. They are so delicious that they will probably not last as long as that!

To make brine the old-fashioned way, continue adding salt to water until you can float an egg in it. Then you will know that you have the correct proportions.

# Whole Olives

Place green olives in salted water – half a cup of salt to each litre of water. Leave for 2 – 3 months. Rinse and place in brine (see above) with lemon slices, garlic and oregano. Use when required.

# Salted Olives
## *Azeitonas de Sal*

2 litres ripe black olives
coarse salt

*Dressing*
5 cloves garlic, crushed or
    chopped

125 ml oil
35 ml vinegar
2 ml ground cumin
10 ml paprika
chopped parsley

Place the olives in an earthenware dish and sprinkle with salt. Leave them for 2 – 3 weeks, until the olives look shrivelled and wrinkled. Remove the olives from the dish, pour boiling water over them and soak them overnight. Drain the olives and rinse in cold water. Drain well, mix with the dressing, and serve. Refrigerate any left-overs.

# Beverages
## *Bebidas*

Portugal produces fine table wines to accompany its

distinctive cuisine, and the wines of Port and

Madeira need no introduction.

To round off a meal it is customary for the men to

have coffee and *bagaceira* (brandy) and for the

women to be served something a little sweeter.

Although many liqueurs can be bought

commercially, it is still traditional to make them at

home. The label 'I Made It' is superior to

even the best-known brands. It is easy to make

liqueurs in Portugal where pure alcohol is

sold over the counter. Locally, one can make liqueurs

using a good cane spirit, brandy or *aguardente*.

# The Wines of Portugal

Portugal is the world's sixth largest wine-producing country. The combination of soil, grapes and climate results in some unique wines from the country's ten officially demarcated wine regions.

The best known Portuguese table wines are the *Vinhos Verdes* (Green Wines), so called not because the wine is green in colour but because of its youth and freshness. The grapes are picked in the early autumn and thus have a low sugar content and a high level of malic acid. The white *Vinhos Verdes* are lemon in colour, have a very low alcohol content and should be served well chilled. The red *Vinho Verde* is not as popular as the white and is an acquired taste. The Bairrada region is famous for its sparkling wines. Rosé wines are very popular – Matheus Rosé is one of the most celebrated rosé wines in the world.

The wines of Port and Madeira need no introduction. The Port wine region was designated as such in 1756 and Madeira has been producing wines since the thirteenth century.

The following are suggestions for wines to serve with different courses:

| | |
|---|---|
| Starters | white Port or Madeira *Sercial* |
| Seafood | oysters and clams: very dry *Vinho Verde* |
| | tuna fish: white *Dão* |
| | *bacalhau* and sardines: red *Dão* |
| Poultry | *Bairrada*, Rosé |
| Red meat | Full-bodied red *Cartaxo* |
| Game | mature red *Dão* |
| Cheese | red Port or Madeira *Boal (Bual)* |
| Coffee | *Aguardente Bagaceira* (Fire Water) |

# Cherries in *Aguardente*
## *Ginjinha*

There are special shops in Portugal (I particularly recall a little one in Lisbon) that sell only *ginjinha*. They have hundreds of bottles and jars of all shapes and sizes filled with this liqueur. You can buy full bottles or just pop in for a tot (rather than a cuppa) while out shopping.

> 1 kg black cherries
> 500 g sugar
> 1 litre *aguardente*

Wash the cherries and, if you wish, remove the stalks. (I leave the stalks on.) Place in a bottle, add the sugar and pour on the brandy making sure that it covers the cherries completely. Spices are sometimes added, such as stick cinnamon or whole cloves. Shake daily for the first few days and then leave for at least one year (sorry about that). It is even better after three years.

# Coffee Liqueur
## *Licor de Café*

> 400 ml boiling water
> 125 ml freshly ground coffee
> 250 g sugar

> 500 ml water
> small strip of lemon rind
> 500 ml brandy

Pour the boiling water over the coffee and leave it to stand for 10 minutes. Strain the coffee. Make a syrup by mixing together the sugar, water and lemon rind. Bring to the boil, simmer for 2 – 3 minutes and then cool. Add the coffee and the brandy. Cover the mixture and leave it for 3 – 4 weeks. Strain and bottle.

# Tim-Tam-Tum

I don't know the origin of the name, but the liqueur is a traditional Madeiran one.

2 kg sugar
25 g stick cinnamon
25 g dry tea leaves *or* 1 teabag
100 g raisins

1 vanilla pod
1 litre water
1 litre alcohol (cane spirit)
1 litre Madeira wine (the older the better)

Place the sugar, stick cinnamon, tea, raisins, vanilla pod and water in a saucepan and simmer for 20 minutes. Add the alcohol and the wine. Cover and leave for 2 – 3 days. Strain and pour into a jar or bottles.

# Aniseed Liqueur
## *Anis*

1 litre *aguardente*
2 ml fennel seed
5 ml aniseed
2 ml coriander seed
5 ml star aniseed
1 ml ground cinnamon

**Syrup**
400 g sugar
500 ml water

Pour the brandy over the spices, cover and leave for 1 week. Add the syrup, made by boiling together the sugar and water, and leave for 2 – 3 weeks. Shake daily during the first few days. Clarify, filter and bottle.

***To clarify liqueurs:*** For each litre of liqueur add one egg white and the crushed shell of one egg. Leave to stand overnight and then strain through filter paper.

# Aniseed Liqueur – a quicker version

1,25 kg sugar
1 litre water
2 egg whites

1 eggshell, crushed
1 litre alcohol (cane spirit)
aniseed essence to taste

Boil together the sugar, water, egg whites and eggshell for 30 minutes. Strain and cool. Add the alcohol and aniseed essence to taste. Leave for 2 – 3 weeks.

# Cognac

I don't know how close this is to the real thing, but do try it.

1 litre sweetened black tea
1 star aniseed
12 dried camomile seed heads

100 g sugar
100 ml Madeira wine
1 litre alcohol (cane spirit)

Place all the ingredients in a large jar for 2 weeks, shaking once a day. Strain and bottle.

## Cocktails

# Caipirinha

As Brazilian as the Copacabana beauties, this is a most refreshing cocktail.

2 lemons (in Brazil limes are used)
25 ml castor sugar
ice cubes
*cachaça* (cane spirit)

Quarter the lemons, chop roughly, and add the sugar. Place in food processor and, using the metal blade, process for 1 minute. Pour the lemon mixture into tumblers. With the machine running, drop ice cubes through the feed tube of the food processor and process for 15 – 20 seconds until crushed. Pour on to the lemon and sugar mixture in the tumblers and top with cane spirit.

# April in Portugal

crushed ice
20 ml white Port
10 ml *aguardente*

10 ml orange juice
5 ml grenadine

Crush the ice and place it in a cocktail shaker with all the other ingredients. Shake well and then strain into a cocktail glass. Decorate with a spiral of orange peel.

# Lisbon at Night
## *Lisboa a Noite*

25 ml *ginjinha*
20 ml aniseed liqueur
5 ml sugar

25 ml orange juice
pinch of ground cinnamon

Place all the ingredients in a cocktail shaker and shake well. Strain and serve with cherries from the *ginjinha*.

# Madeira Cobbler

4 ice cubes
2 peach slices
4 grapes
2 pineapple chunks

10 ml grenadine
1 dash cherry liqueur
1 dash orange liqueur
Madeira wine

Crush the ice and place it in a goblet. Add the fruits, grenadine and liqueurs. Top with Madeira wine and serve with a straw and a spoon.

## Other Beverages

# Sangria

Very popular in Portugal, especially among the younger generation. Did we copy our neighbours, or did they copy us?

| | |
|---|---|
| 1 litre red wine | 100 g sugar |
| 250 ml orange juice | ice cubes |
| 10 ml lemon juice | lemon and orange slices |
| 20 ml orange liqueur | lemonade (optional) |

Place all the ingredients in a large jug. Add the lemonade just before serving.

# Poncha

Typical of Madeira, this drink is usually prepared in a jug in front of the customers. So don't make it just for yourself – invite your friends to join you. A special wooden whisk called a *mexilhao* or *mexelote* is used to mix the drink.

Visit Madeira in the winter. Drive up to Pico do Areiro, 1 900 metres above sea-level, order *poncha* and hope that you will be snowed in.

| | |
|---|---|
| 400 ml cane *(aguardente de cana)* | 75 ml honey |
| 150 ml water | 10 ml lemon juice |
| | 25 ml sugar |

Place all the ingredients in a large jug. Place the handle of the whisk between the palms of your hands and rub your hands until all the ingredients have been thoroughly mixed. Now that you have warmed your hands, drink the *poncha* and warm your heart.

## *Vinho com Pêssegos*

During the summer months it was quite a treat for us, as children, to arrive home from school and find a jug of this delicious refresher in the fridge.

6 peaches
sugar to taste
20 ml Port wine

1 litre semi-sweet white wine
lemonade

Peel and slice the peaches and add sugar to taste. Place in a large jug and add the Port wine and the white wine. Leave for 1 – 2 hours. Add the lemonade just before serving.

# Mulled Wine
## *Vinho Quente*

This is usually served after arriving home from midnight mass. Remember it is winter, and very cold. The oldest male member of the household prepares the wine and the guest-of-honour is served first. It is served in little bowls.

1 bottle Port wine
50 ml *aguardente*
15 ml honey

125 ml raisins
1 stick cinnamon

Place the Port wine in a saucepan. Add all the remaining ingredients, bring to the boil, and serve at once.

# INDEX (Bold type indicates dishes which are illustrated)